A

MW00781666

Volume I

Writings from the Sudden Denouement
Literary Collective

SUDDEN DENOUEMENT
PUBLISHING

Sudden Denouement Anthology Volume I
Copyright © 2018 by Sudden Denouement Literary Collective

Published in the United States of America by Sudden
Denouement Publishing

SUDDEN DENOUEMENT
PUBLISHING

Library of Congress Control Number 2018906514

ISBN 978-0-9990796-3-8

Editors: Jasper Kerkau
                Kindra M. Austin
                Christine E. Ray

Dedication

The authors of the Sudden Denouement Literary Collective would like to dedicate this anthology to our readers, past, present and future. You are our compatriots on a creative odyssey. The knowledge that there is a constellation of individuals with whom our divergent expressions resonate is nourishment for our souls. We write as the outpouring of our very essence, with all of the attendant angst and vulnerability that such divulgence entails. Your compassionate readership and vociferous support holds our work in a place of honor. We are forever grateful to you all, for taking the leap of faith with us as we have walked out upon the ledges of our truths.

Acknowledgements

This monument to the might of the wordsmith was erected with enthusiasm, and keen devotion to the profound art of written expression. It is an honor and privilege to salute the Sudden Denouement Collective—thank you for your sincerity and dedication. An extended thanks to Jimmi Campkin for his generous cover photo contribution.

To the editors: the energy you brought to this endeavor is extraordinary, and much appreciated. Thank you all for your efforts and solid commitment to teamwork.

Editorial Staff
Kindra M. Austin
Richard Crandall
Dennis Earley
Jasper Kerkau
Nicole Lyons
Christine E. Ray
Marcia Weber

Introduction

The brightest light is preceded by darkness. This is certainly true of the two year journey that preceded this collection of work by 29 writers from 7 countries, brought together by a shared urgency to write their truth and to be part of something greater than the sum of its parts. I never anticipated this result two years ago over a shared beer with an old friend amid the ruin of my American dream. Richard Crandall and I sat on a hot spring night in Houston discussing how I could ascend the wreckage of my life. That evening Sudden Denouement was born.

It became clear to me early in this journey that Sudden Denouement would evolve into the literary community that it did. However, I never visualized the launch of a publishing company or the friends I would make all over the world in the search to connect with others like myself. It soon became apparent that this spark that ignited on that Houston night would grow to be much larger than myself or any one person.

Writers are often solitary practitioners, concocting their magic in hidden, quiet places. It has long been the mandate of Sudden Denouement to bring people together in a special way, to come in from the desert, to find a beautiful fellowship that celebrates the brave ones, the renegades, the writers who challenge the norms and don't have a place at the table of polite literary society. We are a collective of divergent literature, an unstoppable force of energy, articulating something that others are afraid to express. Individually and even more so collectively, we push boundaries and carve out a unique place.

This Anthology is a carefully curated compendium of poem, prose, and fiction from our archives, as well as previously unpublished pieces. It truly represents the best of Sudden Denouement. This volume captures the astonishing raw power of our individual and united poetic voices. We have carved out our space in the literary landscape and created home.

I believe that this is only the beginning. Momentum and synergy happen when one writer steps outside of themselves and connects with another who speaks their language. There is something unique and special about the Sudden Denouement experience. It is my honor and privilege to introduce you to our world and I look forward to welcoming you back again and again.

Jasper Kerkau
Founder & Editor in Chief, Sudden Denouement Literary Collective

Table of Contents

15

16

17

I am a F*cking Writer!
Jasper Kerkau

I am a writer!
I sit on the left-hand of the gods and have a special
dispensation to decode the secret, universal rhythms, find
patterns in the whispers which are inaudible to profane
ears. My role is that of an observer; a quiet, meditative
force who has a holy charge to record the divine misery,
the blind mysteries, the eek-and-turn everyday struggle
of life, seen through the eyes of one who has divested
himself of all worldly goods.

Who are you?

I am a fucking writer! I am convicted, given over to the
great purpose of wresting the truth away from the earth,
buried under layers of silt and sediment, caught up in the
swirl of the waters that lean to the great gravitational
forces as the world mercilessly spins in the great
unknown. The curse is the burden, the pulling back the
veil, looking into the languid eyes affixed on the gloss
and glitter of shards of glass and bits of triviality, finding
the gift in otherness, turning away from the doomed, and,
alas, finding a tribe of others who beckon the same call.

What do you do?

I am a writer! Though during the day, I am an
undercover laborer, engaged in the task of finding means
to an end. Looking out of windows, staring at watches,
waiting…waiting for life to begin. The toiling is for

naught; it doesn't define me. I work for a living, but when I put my head on pillow, or look in the mirror, I know exactly what I am. Touched by the hand of god, beholden to vision and in collaboration with a silent minority, hiding out, going through motions, learning, and watching. I am anointed by almighty forces, who picked me up and spit me into the world with love in my heart, to stand in the shadows and pay the price for all of the beauty and all the unhappiness in the world.

Sentence of Sentience
Max Meunier

what have i
but quieted inquiries
hollowed
and echoed
through vales
of a sub-violet druse
of aversion
no tangible touch
to form valid expression
intentions adrift
amid merciless
miles of mutable morass
from which somnolous streams
softly spill
forth eclipses
in lapses
bereft of availing account
where whims slowly waft
beyond walled apparitions
fled from partition
to form in summation
a dormant despair
born of quiet desperation
awaiting conclusion
in sediments muring
a freedom reprieved
of sententious ideal
for what purpose plausible
peers within prisms

but spectacle
cradling consciences captious
enraptured in casting incessant goodbyes
alas
i digress
lest my thoughts
become i

Subjective
Matthew D. Eayre

These words have no meaning.
A metaphor, perhaps,
an impending ice age covering the landscape while I run
from the freeze.
A turn of phrase, it could be, I never wanted anything to
stop my destruction, and she jumped on the grenade to
save me.
A rhyme, to mark the time, the wind brings me a smile,
Thinking of you drinking in that happy place about a
mile
Away from my hands, you can stand on your own and
Find a new home while I wither alone and drink my
lonely tears,
I'm stuck in my fear and will be for years...
These words have no meaning, when they sit on your
screen, on your printed page you read them and translate
into images of your own experience
My life is my own and when I write I feel a release of
captured agony,
Does it reach you?
This man is getting old, trying to find a way to keep
being
I've found a medication that works
Strange eyes see my heart and pass judgement,
this is poetry,
this is not
this is good enough,
this is crap
you're a good writer,

you're a poet
you're an imposter
and you know you don't belong
These words have no meaning
Here I sit, a survivor of countless attempts on my life
(by my own hand)
Here I sit, a remnant of innocence twisted and stolen,
I stand, the thing that grew when a brand-new tree was broken.
These words have a meaning.
I have lived this life and I have tried to find a meaning, I have fought against all of the noise in my head, all of the hate in the world which buries my people.
I have tried to lift hearts from cages and teach birds to walk,
So their wings won't fail them.
These words have meaning.
If you will just see
I cannot yet fly
I have only a wish to know the clouds.
If you will read these words and know my love, we may both find the wind.
I have died and come back to life
to be here
to give you this moment
I write for only one reason.
I am these words.
I have meaning.

On Becoming a Writer
Christine E. Ray

Sometimes, adopting the names 'writer' and 'poet'
led her to encounters with the most amazing minds
connecting her with a larger community
At other times she thought that 'writer' and 'poet'
were the loneliest names she had ever called herself
Waking up every morning
to unzip her chest, her gut
and bare her truths to the world
because like others of her kind
she was complex, messy, containing
multiple truths, not a singular one

Sometimes she felt like she was writing
to a small group of intimate friends
at others times,
she felt like she was calling out her truths
into an empty desert landscape
without even a coyote or armadillo
to hear her words before they fell away
forlorn and unread
unheard and unacknowledged
rendering the writer, the poet herself
invisible, diminished somehow

She was always struck by the juxtaposition
of her physical body negotiating
close suburbs,
crowded subways and jostling city sidewalks
on the way to her day job

while her heart and mind
wandered in the isolated wilderness
while errant words and wisps of dreams
and drops of feelings like rich, red blood
continued to seep out of her

Genesis
Erich James Michaels

A distant diamond's glint at horizon's schism. Gnomus and Sylvestris each claiming victory. For both the mountain's penetration into the sky and the shadowed valley's invasion into the earth. Spur on your antediluvian Andalusian. A wound that won't heal and amnesia's touch. The gloved psychometrist looking to divine a flood that's washes away the cobwebs. Fingers laced into mane you gallop on. You and mount are one in thought and action. Serpentining through boulder and brush. Something you can't remember drives you. Not just in the need to remember, but by something that haunts your unremembered dreams at the periphery. Somehow, you know this with certainty. The closer you get to horizon's diamond, the more it seems a second sun's ascending. To save your sight you approach askew. A purple bruise spreads across the sky and a diamond becomes a city...a city of marble and mirrors. The curtain wall reflects your approach. A haggard horseman on a pale horse. The gate is open and you enter the courtyard. Sounds of meals and conversations echo, but not a soul to be seen. You're amazed at how everything is so polished. Stars shimmer on the polished obsidian floor and you watch a raven pass between you and the gibbous moon. You stable your horse and seek out an inn. Brought to a dining hall by the din within, you enter. You're immediately struck by how incredibly beautiful everyone is. Stunning. As you walk through you quickly notice that no one is registering your existence. Almost as if you were invisible. Frustrated you lean directly in

27

front of a man who could pass for Adonis, and the slightest micro-expression of disgust flashes across his face, then just as quickly you are invisible again. You feel yourself being pulled back. Surprised, you turn to find a silver ghost gently pulling at your wrist. In a state of confusion you follow the mirrored apparition. You're led through a door that blends into the back wall. Once through, the specter sheds its skin and a young man appears from beneath the reflective fabric. He hangs his quicksilver cloak on a peg and scurries off to join a whole crew of workers. You watch as they all wrap up the nights festivities. The plating of desserts and the washing of dishes. Some are working mortar and pestle, adding botanicals to river clay and purified water. A part of their God's nightly regimen, you are told. When all is taken care of, everyone files outside the city through a hidden door. It is here, where everyone really comes alive! Constellations form from bonfires across the hillside. People are pulled into orbits with likeminded folk about these man made suns: musicians; singers; dancers; acrobats; painters; sculptors; weavers, and so many more. The old teaching the young with such joy. Wandering, however, you come across a family that isn't participating in any festivities. Instead, you find a couple doting on a young child. They wait on him hand and foot, primping and preening, cooing and soothing. You move in closer to find the most adorable little girl. Dressed in fabrics that look out of place in this hillside gathering, hair done formally, and a hint of makeup. She catches sight of you, smiles and begins to stir. Her parents glance at you, immediately assessing, and with the same snarl of distaste you witnessed earlier, they correct the girl. She is now placid and you are, in this moment, a ghost. You

28

wander off, thinking on the genesis of a god. Shaken from your thoughts, you are whisked away. You are stripped down and ushered into a copper tub that sits on glowing embers. Three or four people move about you, and as one places cucumber slices over your eyes, you are enveloped in embryonic warmth and darkness. Not knowing your past you wish to be born anew. You hear the giggles and talk of years of dirt, and wondering what lies beneath. You feel your long hair being scissored and creams being applied to your face, as you drift off. When you awake, you find yourself sitting in a chair, fully dressed, your hand slides along freshly shaven chin, then removes a hot towel draped across your face and the cucumber slices. When you open your eyes you are surrounded. Smiles falter to looks of reverence and people begin genuflecting. Confused, you look around. Finding a mirror beside you on the chair, you bring it up with shaky hand. You find beauty in that mirror, but without memory it is a stranger's face. Nevertheless, you are pulled in and it takes actual effort to lower the mirror to your side. Looking about, you see no eyes will meet your own, save two. The little girl. She gives you a nod of acceptance. The energy coming off everyone else is palpable and for a moment you bask in it. A single tear rolls down your cheek and in one fell swoop you break the mirror on the chair, grab a shard, and drag it down the side of your face. The pain is instantaneous, but in that moment before passing out, you see a half-smile play across the little girl's mouth, then screaming.

You walk out onto the hillside, making your way to what has become your bonfire. Fingers tracing the scar along your face. You are greeted by friends. Here you sit, with notebook in hand. You read your latest poem. You describe the shadows that lurk in the recesses of your mind, from former lives forgotten. You are a poet. You are a writer without a past, who has found a new home— the only one you will ever truly know. Here you will weave your backstory and make yourself whole again.

Sister Salty
Marcia Weber

I am salt of the earth
caked in tracks of the tears
wept by oceans
upon weary shores.
I am granularized granite
lodged as fungal spores
between the toes
and among the souls
of all who trespass
here. doting dowagers
crinkle their noses wrinkled
when I stick
beyond the brushing off.
I am powdered moondust
residue of a resurrection
silvering towheaded
locks of touted toddlers.
crushed, vaporized
or trod upon
I glitter on

What can I give you?
Iulia Halatz

What can I give you? I am the blue
as imagined by a blind
and the roots of knowledge
as watered by a scholar.
I am the yellow
wind and the mauve
respond of light
perched
in the ubiquitous trees
tethered in the clouds
that barely scratch
the sky.
I am the green
storm and colorless waves
that wished upon a mountain
to break water in tryst
with the sun.
Not by blindness
we can reorder colors
but by the painting of a soul
in a moment tender
as the liquid moon
is quivering above the forest.

birds & h e a r t s
Ra'ahe Khayat

we're not humans without h e a r t s
but hearts without bodies,
being fed to strange birds
with s t r a n g e r heartbeats-
that nibble on our veins,
and pluck at our skins
until their beaks bleed,
and they h a n g themselves
from a ghost of our r i b s.

1.

Samantha Lucero

a city map is sewn in the scalp;
looped in the goat-milk, or spit out,
tongued in silky blades of stomped
down grass.

i'm crowned with high-pitched fingers
clenched in fur.
in octaves only shades can bear, i simmer
in their holy cradles.
i become the roughened corner of a mouth
grinning at its own joke.

there, the receding home in ranch-style polaroid's of a
dirty blond stranger and my mother squinting in the sun;
some home not mine or yours.
ventricles, which
in a woman's left grows tiny,
and in a man's more supple.
i keep alive by milking goats.

some like lifelines, some like ulcers
the city streets are braided in my hair.

Conflagration
Nathan McCool

From among rampikes where I study ancient things,
I think I could reach up with my ponderosa arms and
pull down all the gods. I could bring them
here to earth, but people would only know them as
madness…
Know them in that same way that the
general population will always know
beauty and brilliance.
I'm society, some things are outside of it;
and gazes are always turned to those things
like the barrel of a gun. Scoffs are shot from
perfect, lipstick painted mouths like bullets.
But to be perfect is to have never burned.
Things that have not endured burning cannot
give light. And in the absence of light,
no one ever sees anything.
What I'm saying is, each person can set themselves afire
in some way and endure –
can be stars speckled against darkness.
To be or not to be is a question of suicide,
but I ask, "To march in bright, radiant, conflagrant
madness…or to simply spectate
in dull content?"
The thing to really remember is:
If you are to spectate, it is only because
more enkindled "mad" things allow it.

for e. d.
Lois Linkens

the city glitters after dark,
busy busy night-owls
shuffle and scuffle
in their white-glass nests.
and we watch,
tired eyes and heavy bags
on a faraway train
we are sexless soulmates
and brotherly brides,
platonic partners pledged
in the ink of mutual need
and searching hearts
sisters in arms,
rosy-cheeks and high-school charms;
my curly-haired comic
heads full of homework,
a makeshift skyline
of yet-to-be
paints itself across the dark,
as young love
rings it's soon-forgotten bell
confused youth;
a cloud-grey gosling
peeks its ugly head
through the bulrushes
to see the swans;
we are cast-away boats
in stormy seas,
just looking for a place to land.

Dream catcher never understood the bus schedule
Mick Hugh

The library has been converted into classrooms for fifth-year students. Shelves emptied and rearranged to fit rows of desks, projector screens, faculty offices and the Office of Student Retention. My exam is running late to complete. I am tapping fingers on the desktop nervously rapping away. My feet twitch uncomfortably. I scribble out essays and vague answers to questions I can only half-read. I don't have the time. I don't have the time and this afternoon you're boarding a bus for a move to LA. It's your mistake; you're my mistake: I let you mistake me. I'm coming with you. I should. I spring from my desk and let the stapled papers fly apart through the air at the professor's head. The race is on skip the elevator and dash the stairs, leave the books behind at the counter I'll come back for them later if they really mean that much to me. I burst out the doors and check the time on my phone – bright fresh sun, and the aluminum numbness creeping deeper in my lower gut; I know I'm going to be late. I hustle across campus and halfway there double-back the other way; in my haste I made the mistake of trying to cut through the campus construction. But all I find in the other direction are new dormitories and expansions under construction for the new Department of Student Retention and I cannot find the god damned parking lot where it used to be.

Out of breath sucking wind through the sweat and jello'd legs, the aluminum numbness has crept up and blossomed into wilting fireworks of frustration and shame – standing alone on the curb sucking wind, just in time to see the bus trail away. Just a moment too late.

Dream catcher, forever just a moment too late.

I've awoken at a desk. Lifeless fluorescent lighting and drool puddled by the keyboard. The office is a warm fuzz of processors and clacking keyboards. Assignments due before the evening commute home, and three hours wasted in a sleep-haze fading out and in, out and in – lonely headlights passing through fog of an empty exurban town. I am standing at dusk at the bus stop with an aluminum numbness curdling my gut. I don't know the time. But I don't know the time. There was something I missed, and it still runs unleashed from my grip, ten years now past my prime. I don't know if the bus is late or if I missed its final run for the day. I may not be home tonight. I may not ever be home again

in time to pay our taxes, or to consolidate our student debt.

Or to find a house to live in,

to keep us off the street.

In time to see the kids grow up,

or in time to grow old with you,

I can't come home again. Ten years of shame and pain puts no hope to death by stone. Alone, and ripped at the

38

heart, I will sit on this bus stop bench and wait for the late-night bus ride back to the dreams that could've been.

bow Wow
Georgia Park

I want the TSA
to smash my dog's
little safety box into bits
instead of just the disposable lock
made especially for smashing
after the thirteen hours she spent in it
in cargo far from my place in the cabin
and then after landing
I hear her cries, desperate
but I'm not be able to touch her
until we clear customs

I free her in Chicago
and dump her into the car
someone brings for us
painstakingly prearranged
I don't count on the headache
the pressure the dog fur
out of reach

someone brings the car for us
to drive back in my homeland
after three years locked out of it
the chatter on the radio sounds foreign
American accented English
-it's hard to listen-

Driving in America is different.
I bow to every driver who passes

like a good Korean
and then I start nodding…
it's the 24 hour difference
I just can't manage
my dog is alive
and I am so
bone tired….

The forest fell from the sky

Jonathan O'Farrell

(Melo – phoenix days)
My foot strides again, over even regular municipal cobbles.
Oh that we had time for civic pride, dear Melo.

Catching up my mind's eye,
breath-taking,
aghast, imagination fails
And;

The non accommodating cafe chairs now suffice;
for although reclining cats
by the 'Castelo' passage
still pose,
the grid and a currency of electrons became useless that night
of the furnace wind.
Not that they needed mobile telecoms the felines, just Bombeiros.
The cats needed mobility, too close to the fire, fur!

It strikes me hard, the light, the dark
and many shades convergent.
Not so subliminal, charcoal.
You can have it back now, your town
'any colour,
so long as it's black',
or, ashen grey at a pinch!

Torches, hairbrushes, a table, art, tool handles, wind up
radios, pencils.
All, or most, Incendiary food,
need I say more?

Another cuddle with a scruffy friend some consolation,
as we navigate now primeval carbonised slopes.
Ruefully I survey a spot with forested mountainsides,
between night barking dogs
and intimacy.
Charred, jet black giesta stubs adorn the place,
where I might have called it forest home.
That arson night the accelerant intoxicated forest,
rained incandescent offerings,
on the innocent in their nightclothes.
The firestorm proclaimed, 'Trajectory Lottery';
have a tidy roof over your head? – Not any more!

And still we my gentle watchers and I
are knowing of quiet celestial bodies
and fiery characters, all in time and rotation.
Good people, not perfect, but good, struggle.

The remote prospect of novel non-religious house front
tiling,
seems to recede, just a little,
In the sooty face of trauma.
No space in the stable this season.
Actually, no stable.
Give me a hammer with a shaft in situ, nails.
Oh, and yes, timber, again.
Then stable.

Auto-estrada,
autopista,
autoroute,
Autobahn, this time
compass pivots north-east,
but, will swing back, again.

Hide and Seek

Daffni Gingerich

I have poured out the contents of my insides today. I don't want them back but there will come a day when they're handed back to me with side notes and red ink. And I will retreat under the bed like I did as a child during hide and seek. There's knowledge left under beds from those who never survived hiding. My eyes would dart back and forth and my heart would race as if death was truly on the outside waiting. It was always the big brown eyes of my brother that found me. And with such a rush I'd demand he be seeker again. He'd whine and I'd ignore him until he quit and we went our separate ways. Headstrong. That's what they call me. I'm hard to stick around because anyone without passion bores me and anyone with it, well, that's deadly. Deadly, like hide and seek. I've had an insatiable craving for sweets lately. I do my best to be an adult and pair them with more salads, but that amount of eating can be too much. I'd need more than 3 salads a day, and three is quite a lot already. If only hiding under the bed brought me sweets, I'd have been more likely to give my brother a turn to hide.

Proper Disturbia
Mick Hugh

I've again picked the wrong major, ten minutes into the second class I can already tell that – this isn't the scene for me. Black cashmere, Eddie Bauer plaids; retro Doc Martens, soft spoken emotions: your poetry better enunciate pulpy vulnerabilities. The Professor has asked me to share my thoughts and my diaphragm spasms a smile. I am trying not to laugh. Because what I've written down is absurd and too honest to be expected, my thoughts here transcribed for our homework assignment. My thoughts on Tennessee Williams', A Streetcar Named Desire. The room is silent and serious in its all-ears respect of my turn to speak. I am having a hard time not laughing. I compose myself. I begin to read.

"A Streetcar revolves around the personal absurdities of three individuals forced to live in close quarters. The main protagonist, Blanche, is [silent laugh] definitely a lunatic." I bite my tongue, deep breath quivering stifled laughter. They are expecting something serious, intellectual, insightful [inward laugh]. I sigh and compose myself, begin again.

"The reason we find this drama an authentic representation of human life [pause to suppress laughter] each character is defined by contradictions," which reminds me of the absurdity at the bottom of the page [face twists to hold in laughter]. BIG BOLD phrases towards the bottom of the page. Breathe, clear my head, begin again.

"The entire drama is founded on the dichotomies of social stratification, intra-personal relationships, and psychological," [laughter, uncontrollable childish laughter shaking my body]. I am screaming, roaring red-faced boisterous laughter. I am being stared at, glared at, all the more to laugh at the unexpectedness and disapproval of this laughter I've kept bottled.

"I'm sorry [laughter, tears-on-my-face laughter]. I'm sorry I can't [indomitable laughter]. I can't help it!" Why so serious? Hahaha! Hahaha!

"Mr. – " starts the professor. "If you have to excuse yourself – "

I collect my books and notebooks into a pile on my desk, peals of laughter coming to a rest: I feel now almost blissful from being caught in this cataract of unyielding laughter. I think – they have no idea what I find so funny and this laughing so flies in the face of expected decorum that it's –

Tremors in my diaphragm I begin to laugh again. My head bangs back, bright clouds of laughter to the ceiling frame a word bubble: "He blew his head off! [laughter like bursts of flak] Her husband! She was this [laughter] precious Southern Belle [laughter] inadvertently [laughter] she inadvertently made him [laughter] blow his fucking head off!" [laughterlaughterlaughterlaughter].

I am no longer taking English 106.

Reflectors.

S.K. Nicholas

You. Her. She. The bottle and a banshee and a priest. A will-o'-the-wisp and the gleam of painted lips all puckered up and ready for the kiss. No poetry and then a little poetry. No women and then your image that comes sauntering into view behind the back of my blacked-out eyes. In schools, they preach hide the soul, and then work comes along and drills it in a little deeper. But art liberates, and good art is the answer to all that ails us. So maybe take me by the hand and walk these streets with me until we can't feel our feet, yeah? Maybe if you want you'll come along with me on a journey someplace strange until we can't remember who we were to begin with, yeah? Maybe you'll let me want you, and the more my heart burns as a result, the more you'll see that these visions I preach are as real as it gets. I ain't proper and I ain't well, and this mouth is far too quiet for its own good, but in my bones, there's darkness and more darkness and this darkness comes as easy as the sleep of reason the rest of them try so hard to deny. There are butterflies mixed with sleeping pills and your trimmed pubic hair I run my tongue over even though the pain itches me something rotten. There's dust on your windowsill and coffee in your belly and wonder smeared all over your pretty little chin of which I bite and chew until you beg me to stop. Chrysalis and fire. June bloom and fairground highs and the smell of cotton candy mixed with hotdogs as lovers stand on the brink. That first kiss. That first touch when fingers long to creep. Those brown eyes and autumn hearts- the two things I seek more than anything. But only God can make a tree, so who I am? My reflection and your reflection, so many reflections and all these reflections that keep on reflecting, oh, how I want them now. So many obsessions and afflictions and addictions and sensations and I wanna feel them all. Let me mirror you and then mirror me back until we're mirrored through and through. Let these reflections keep on reflecting until we screech and howl and our words dissolve and what's left is but a reflection that keeps on reflecting, over and over again.

Broken
Oldepunk

some of us are just broken
born of dust and little disappointments
bleak barrow bones and lamented jewels
made of helpless tears and midnight fears
saltpeter and cobwebs, nickel and newt
lost toys that cost joy
cast of glass and weakness
the forlorn reborn in submission
forced into place even when
the pieces never fit
a cross-threaded screw
muck on the sandal of a forgotten god
a chewed up pen
dull pencil with no eraser
primer painted wagon
with busted wheels
many things of little use
an alchemical composition
turning gold to lead,crack and peel
the Narcissist stone!
you do not understand
as the dead envy the living, so
do the broken hate the anointed, you
as i hate you
as I hate myself
the chipped stone defacing a masterpiece
mold on the Monet
dry rot in the wall
asbestos in the halls

toxic relations and divorces
aria of dissonant discourses
some of us are just broken
one of the unchosen
I am the name it always hurts to say
the reflected shadow at the window pane
you will recall we just were
not the same
the broken one will eat the blame
cherry wood ashes and goat's hair
shell casings and a hangman's prayer
the puzzle with the missing pieces
a chill wind that never ceases
bitter pills and wounded pride
all of the shit you try to hide
the hateful words that were spoken
these are the desolate ways

we are broken

A Drift of Dead Comics
N. Ian McCarthy

You lay, balanced flat across the colonnade of my
fingers. A lower-left corner wags with the intervallic
oscillation of a floor fan—the limb of a cotton bed sheet,
straddling a clotheswire in the wind. You are almost a
breathing thing: the impulse of a contracting diaphragm.
You are the sucking gill of an angled fish, one who
cannot oxygenate without water. My wax lips strain
around the vowels of an invented dialect, during the
seventh minute of my resistance to pick at the flat-folded
staples that run up the split of your faulted spine. Do I
engender a quake that will defoliate your season of
autumn? Can I scatter your sheets like loose cedar
shavings, as mulch for the bed of my own Silk Road?

I am the yellow-eyed cat, lean and starved, who ladles
the spoon of his tongue into the dish of the remainder of
your souring cream. I mount a low mangrove branch to
bay into the charcoal square of your nighttime doorway.
Come not for me or for anyone. You are a reliquary of
mutable fictions, and you behoove no further corporal
appearances.

Are you more than the sum of your linearly arranged
innards—this cardboard box lined with plastic sleeves
and white splints to keep your keepsakes from creasing?
Are you only your cut-to-fit pages printed in four-color
process? Value is a future thing, fuzzy, until the future
appraises it. I hold you by your edges and delicately, like
a cautious amateur rolling through brittle Egyptian

papyrus. And, in the ball of this lamplight, I become a tonsured vulture who stabs the vice of his beak into a gob of your dried rib meat.

Six years ago, I misplaced my hat at a bar ringed by soot-black acres of potato dirt, where notes of vinegar from a nearby canning plant punctuated the inferences of my nose. It was a driving cap, sewn with a damask label boasting *Donegal Tweed* on the bowl of its belly. The memory of its passing is an ash steeped in smudgy tumblers of neat whiskey—as all things that transpire while drunk are contractually forfeited upon embarkation. The recently tangible became only a murmur in the chill of my morning baldness. Am I more than those thick, raspy hands? The ones that likely scrubbed over its green-and-brown woven fibers? Is there any molecule of *me* still stitched into the band of its fit? Or do I become a novelty, minus all personal history, as is the fate of any found and inherited thing? Do I exist in a green garbage pile, awaiting my delivery unto the heap? Or am I hung lightly on a wood knob, in the corner of room buoyed by festive music?

May the serialized volumes of my being—like yours—be bound in clear plastic sheaths and filed horizontally by issue number, their values cataloged and fondled by speculators. In my collection, a body-warm cap, tumbled from the crown of a quite common skull. Worth a fuzzy thing, indeterminate without precise coordinates in space and in time. Permanence is a windblown page printed in chalk.

Divine
Nathan McCool

It's all been Russian roulette and the game
was rigged from the start. So,
you dear and distant god, what am I to
make of these small moments between
the hammer and the head?

Allow me this thought:
The clouds that are expelled from me
into winter's dusk no longer take the form
of myth or fancy as they are painted
against a dying sun. They are cotton candy
caricatures of a man in the act of
self immolation.
I believe perhaps all of this has been a walk
down Saigon Road, and I'm now coming to sit calmly
without movement or sound at this intersection

The world I have seen is a nuclei, and
I am an electron in sporadic oscillation all around it.
I may leave at any given moment to bring
the clouds of another world to wholeness
or part from them to expose them to the
ultra violence of ultraviolet light.

Because I no longer know what I'm really staying for.
To witness war or the loss of love?
To watch children absorbed into the earth
or for them to wander off from innocence
into the people they will become?

At this point I no longer truly think of ends,
just the momentum of the moment.
I'll one day have a grave like a laceration
upon the flesh of the earth,
and you'll all pour me in like salt.
But that is a moment with no meaning for me.

But in existence,
where misery takes up residence in my bed
so often I've taken to calling her "baby",
I am an entity and an element.
In existence, I have lost more than I have
ever received; and carry more demons
than I do pores of my skin.

Nothing out there cares if I got my druthers,
but I'll let you know:
If you were to force me to live this innumerable times,
I'd sink these jagged teeth into life
all over again.

Us
S.K. Nicholas

There's junk food in my belly and a book on Ian Brady in my hand. Blinking my eyes, the pages are stained with sweat and splashed with spit. Remember when I would take you from behind and how I'd lean over and tell you to turn your face and look me in the eyes? How I'd get you to open your mouth so I could let a stream of saliva drip onto your tongue? You don't? Well, shame on you. Somewhere in my mind, the smell of stale beer drifts to me across playing fields. It's autumn, and the leaves are crisp and crumble in my hands before falling to the floor like confetti. There's a chill kick in the breeze that pains my face whenever I shave. There are bus journeys and newsagents that sell sweets and magazines with free toys attached to their covers. There are coffee shops and pet stores and underpasses where children from nearby schools paint pictures of the world they live in. After a drunken night out in town with friends, I walked home alone and took a leak in that underpass, and as my yellow stream of piss splashed the colourful buildings they had painted, I laughed until my stomach hurt. That book on Ian Brady, I keep it in my bag and read it in the shade of trees and weeds far from the presence of others. His voice is one of existence, and as such, it reminds me that I exist. In silence is where I grow, and yet in your arms is where I'm alive more than ever. I'm not sure how that works, and that's part of the problem. There's a cigarette to ease my troubles and to make my head spin. There's a song that connects us even though so many days have been and gone in between our last kiss. For some, the meaning of words is a thankless one, but for me, God is in every letter. This poetry. This sense of glory. There is nothing that comes close save for the image of you leaving footprints on fresh snow, or the taste of your neck as we do our thing while trying so hard to resist the breaking of dawn. And to think of all those buildings where our ghosts dance in silence, and to think of those fields where I would carry you because it was too muddy and you didn't want to get your shoes dirty. Those dead cigarettes of mine, they are still there somewhere, along with those empty bottles of wine I would fling into the mouth of the quarry. And that hairclip you lost- that too is there. Everywhere we go and have been, there are artefacts that hold so much meaning the rest will never be able to fathom. What's gone is not lost, and what's not lost is with us every step of the way.

Still
Mitch Green

Vagrant contagious blur,
bludgeoned pastel in ripe
maturity on the wire of
mental poverty.

Breathing, still

we peddle pleasure to
charm the mousy, paper
white wives rapt in inert
rifts of the vanished.

But, still

to them we are nothing, but gravel
in the making of scars.

Still breathing,
breathing still.

Of the Sword Blade in the Sun
Jonathan O'Farrell

Some unstoppable truths.

A sword blade has two sides.

The craft of sword making is an old one.

It takes many true and uncompromising elements to make an excellent sword, the right metal, the dark matter that is elemental carbon, white heat of the fire, cleansing waters.

The sword, a strong and mostly unstoppable implement of war, it has two sides. Without both sides it is nothing, not sharp, not honed, not fit for purpose, be it war, defence, or peace keeping.

But when it is strong, true and honed it has unmistakable purpose. And that purpose is not stopped by shields, maybe delayed, but not stopped, ever. As long as there is the strength of life in the arm that wields it, it will do its work.

Hold it up in the air, against an intense sunlight. If it be held broad side, you may see it. If it be held cutting edge facing into the sun, you may not see it. But at least in the radiant and uncompromising white light of day, you have a chance of seeing it, in all its very final glory.

A sword wielded in the dark of the night is the most dangerous, even to the hand on the shaft of it.

Be it either side of blade, day or night; done with skilled swordsmanship, or blindly thrust, in the dark, by a near do well, the result to the tender and open parts, at its journeys end, are the same, grievous injury, or death.

Wishing all parts of your being true honourable strength, wisdom and light.

Under the sun.

Modest Phantom
Mitch Green

Haunted thin. Another malefactor
in the tabernacle of sober innocence.
Sheathed inward, between a soiled
pair of linen and wood, the man in
black wool bares illuminant eyes.
Secrets stacked on the forehead of
monstrous oppression; a catalog criminal.
Smokey cocks sifted through fragments
of mien – detoxing the nimble phantom
in nothing. Modest bones knew how to
collapse, inhaling tufts of fur.
The colorless beauty.
The iron warmth of man.
The living lore of Lilith.

Been Bloody
Richard Crandall

Terror fills the streets
in dark
as we cry to ourselves
sleep at night
you don't know me
anymore
How many days how many nights
when we pull out
hair
and scratch out
eyes
Done seen too much
the information is relentless
I didn't have a choice
won't make it
you gave me the gun
tried to make it
right
She was standing there
right in front of him
and all i can see
is red
red red red
And i can't wash it
clean
i can't take it
away
we both are
still here

bloody

Sabotage
Mitch Green

An angular arena of
mortal suspiria imitates
the silk hollow bedding
of watery eyed,
venomous shapes.

Sabotage the salty ache
in cathartic bones to
keep sailing veins.

Absolve in awe,
the glass caves
eaten by
dynamite.

We are all the
animals of god with
made up names in
places we *don't belong.*

Burning at the Stake

Richard Crandall

when you're sure in your ways
no one can tell you
the truth
and we're right at all costs
as desperation sets in
when I'm cornered and pinned
is when you feel no shame
you look unsure of yourself
let me give you a hand
let me open the door
help me to understand
when I'm engulfed in the blaze
no one will tell you why
and we've struggled and lost
desperation's a friend
and they are smiling at me
because
its the
end

Glass Poison
Mitch Green

edgy knives
surgeon the
Conscious
thread.

some people
are coffins; a
contagious
casualty shiver.

glassy fish in
poison punch.

worming husky
women.

Pool Party
Jasper Kerkau

At some point, towards the end of the night, I get into the pool with my clothes on. Adults are on the patio talking in hushed tones about divorce and lost nights from the early-nineties. Kids laugh and squeal, chasing each other through the house and around the pool. I hold my breath and float to the bottom, thinking of the mess I have to clean up. *My life is falling apart.* I gave my debit card for someone to get orange juice an hour ago. I ponder this and pull myself back up and repeat the process several times meditating on the mess, the residue from ribs, beer bottles, mistakes, dead ends. Eventually I sit on the edge of the pool and try to light a cigarette. My fingers are wet. The cigarette breaks. *My f'ing luck!* My son waves with a big smile, he is elated. *I love you daddy.* I lean over and hug his small, wet frame in the pool. My mind races. *I have to get up. I have to get up. Everything will be okay. Everything will be okay.* Eventually the house empties. I put the kids to bed and darkness washes over me. There is no path. I have to start over tomorrow. I have to keep moving.

Haunted House
Nathan McCool

The doorway
has become dissociative. Things may
enter or leave without being taken notice
of in the slightest.
They will come to find the piano shuddering,
it's teeth chattering and it's body oddly
formed into a fetal position all huddled up
in a cocoon of drunken catharsis.
The paintings, they have become severely
bipolar and are beginning to melt
like naked candles fused to the window
looking outside and offering the false perception
that it is safe to wander between these walls. The Walter
Anderson's and the Dali's,
the Van Gogh's and the junkyard salvages; they
no longer know which expressions
are proper for making love, greeting strangers,
or for killing with their bare hands. And
the skeletons that hang from the
ceiling, they are entirely hysterical. They sing
long echoing lullaby's and longer goodbyes
through a bass amp buried below them
and are often interrupted by laughter at
their small plights – their sexual organs
turning to dust and the chaffing of the
string that tethers them to this place.
Somewhere here there is a bed
plagued with anxiety and night terrors.
And on it a man with a guitar plays

a song about suicide
with a beer bottle as a pick. And any tears
in this moment, spilling even down to the
tattoos that beg you to read their ideals,
they are the purest of things; the least
haunted by disease or disorder.

I am the cracked walls and leaky ceiling.
I am the vengeful specter.
I am everything here.

Visitors are so fond of saying what resonates in this
domain
is either ghostly or sibylline.
But, if you were to know the history
of this ancient vessel,
you would know it is only sublimely human
in all its love
and its capacity for great suffering.

Slow Day.
S.K. Nicholas

Stood on the corner of the block, here comes a gust of wind and a wave of empty crisp packets that speak to me of the hole in my life that just can't be filled. Waiting head down and oblivious, here comes the pain of aching kidneys and a bellyache that reminds me of why it's a good thing to drink in moderation, but moderation breeds complacency, and that just spells the end. Sometimes, I get this romance in me for a way of living that sidesteps the useless shit others find so appealing, and then I remember why detachment is my whore. No one to answer to, and no one to let down, just my baby doing what I want, no questions asked. I mean, who wants to strive for a vision no one else is willing to believe? Who wants to be ridiculed for only wishing to stay true to oneself? There's an ache in my left arm that won't shift, and I've only got a single cigarette to last me until I get home, which could be hours at this rate. Should've bought a new pouch earlier in the evening, but laziness got the better of me, so I had to scrub one together from all the loose tobacco in my satchel. Yeah, a satchel. *And what?* There's poetry in the small things, and a sense of beauty that comes simply from being open and in tune with the universe without fear of being left hanging. But misanthropy is my one true love, and I won't ever quit her, because she won't ever quit me. Without realising, I've missed my bus, and right on cue, here comes the rain. It flattens my hair and does its best to kill my cigarette, but against God's best wishes, I keep the fucker burning by lunging into the doorway of a store that's been empty since before I was born. Keeping an eye on the traffic that moves before me, absence finds me and kisses my neck. The ghosts of my childhood. The ghost of you. Sometimes, when I'm drunk and drifting off to sleep with the TV on, I wish to join them. Wish to get back and get out. But this thing needs seeing through to the end, because what else is there but to admit defeat like those that came and went without leaving so much as a mark. The next bus takes its time, but eventually it appears, and so I journey from town to town looking out the window at places I'll never step foot and never miss, and it don't mean a thing, because I've got this vision, and this vision takes me places they wouldn't believe.

Can't
Pbbr

Can't sleep lately. Everything's too bright. I'm not used to serenity; I am comfortable in the moss, under a rock, in the onyx flames of ill repute. Where light burns black with a perfect pitch, a neglected bastardized stinging glitch, oily but warm. Someone came along and snuffed the blackness. It's too bright in this room. I want to go back to sleep, but not for as long as I will if I do.

Can't breathe lately. The air's too clean. Septic breath of a lurid death is what I crave. Putrid stench, nostalgic days. Comfort food like mom used to make, wasp nest chili and seaweed pizza. The old familiar sting of glass in broken nostrils, coppery fragrant like dead wood. Stink of shit and honeysuckle. But someone came along and brought fresh flowers with them. Not the offensive ones; the gorgeous odor of peace. And they make me uneasy.

Can't talk lately. Not much to berate. I was a stuttering forlorn chicken in a filthy cage, squawking frothing castrated rage. But someone came along with lozenges. Nothing left to scratch and bark. I'm afraid of silence. I'm afraid of mellow golden diatribes, the lack of violence. What happened to screaming at a wall? You're safe inside, and you know it. And I can't get to you, and you know I regret it.

Can't love lately. It's a stagnant slab of cheery smiles, a vagrant loft of airy lies, laid out before me. Everyone is happy. Let's all be sociable. Let's dance with other people's wives to bubblegum pop, not too close. Leave a void between, the façade of trust and happiness. The empty spaces where attraction used to fit. Deceit, defeat, unseat, complete. Treat me to a stabbing orgasm of penile snap. What the fuck is this trust shit.

Can't die lately. And it's making me uncomfortable.

Dust

Matthew D. Eayre

Touch and go, for awhile, it was
Lives hanging from scales which tip
one way, then the other
Waiting to be saved
from gravity's promise
the hands of ghostly gods
clutch in futility and gain no purchase.

Once, light beams led the way through
no more, not meant to be
Once, hope whispered of glory
or sacred peace
or love

No more

Faces in clouds of memory drift
and taunt our weary hero,
his shoulders slumped and his eyes
unable to weep,
though miles of mourning flowers
mark his passage

Once, fear held blades and bullets
slicing and blasting away
a facade of curiosity

No more, not afraid
never again

Once, pleasure tortured dreams
soaked sheets and blankets,
left wanting in the daylight

No more

Once, more than once,
a thousand times,
imagined trysts and fantasized rendezvous with death and
the sun
blocked out clarity

No more

I Survived the Storm

Jasper Kerkau

I survived the storm. Watched everything explode and evaporate in the slow waters of time, billowing out of the dirty earth, inching up sidewalks, devouring curbs, and quiet lives. It all goes away so quickly, the boring conversations, the Sunday afternoons, and fried chicken, the little lives of misery, heaped into the darkness, left silent in dusty rooms, soaked and miserable. Civility and comfort are all so fleeting. I shed the rain, the moon, the failures and regrets, bury heart and words under the pillow. I give them their leisure, and I take a million crosses and deformed shrines, puked up the unnatural pleasures and, alas, have all the pain.

I survived the storm. Molding my stars, peeling off the television and cycles of vomit and bile filtering through every fiber of my being. It is theirs; it is not mine. I will run in circles for eternity, eat fire, and resign myself to the arms of a beautiful girl with a big heart. I stuff mediocrity and resentment in empty potato chip bags and give back to the earth, hoping it will be recycled the next time around. A one-thousand-year event. A speck in time. A sneeze and cough on the big toe of forever. I will eat the water out of hand, starve no more. Drive away dark clouds and find the golden rainbows in my heart. Everything will be okay this time. The sun will come out, and it will all go away.

Raven
Christine E. Ray

It starts as tightness
tingling
across bare shoulder blades
becomes an itch
I can't quite reach
stretch my spine sinuous
slow
vertebrae by vertebrae
long for a shot of whiskey
or three
liquid gold disinhibition I can blame
for the reckless choice
I am about to make
I finally let go
tightly coiled control
gasp with relief
as I finally unleash the darkness
onyx feathers rip
sharp and true through the flesh of my back
talons shoot from fingertips
toes
bones burned hollow
by demon fire dwelling in my belly
exquisite pain of rebirth
brings me briefly to my knees
I arise something new
wipe the blood from my mouth
spread fledgling wings
and with the lift of the north wind

I claim the night sky
mine

Beneath

Erich James Michaels

I need a sensory deprivation tank
Where I can practice mindfulness
I want to peel away the layers
I want to be present
In the moment
Without any sensory input
No light, no sound
Completely out of touch
To remember that the outer
Is created by the inner
I want to gaze into the abyss
And not care if it gazes back
I want to deprive my mind
To the point of Ganzfeld effect
From nothing to something from nowhere
Through the doors of perception
I'll step through with abandon
And when I've finally had my fill
I'll climb out
Towel dry myself off
And feeling the void
The spaces
Between nucleus and electrons
The beneath
The emptiness within reflected
I'll face the world untethered
Unafraid

The Mmm of Her
Nicole Lyons

I was convinced she was crazy
and I couldn't stand the pitch of her voice
but for the way she would say, "Mmmm"
when I told her about the thoughts,
and how they pummeled me darkly.
I liked the Mmmm of her, the way
it brought out the whites of her eyes,
and I wondered as they closed
if they were watching her thoughts
as closely as they watched mine.
And I wished to poke at them,
her thoughts not her eyes,
although I would be lying if I said
I hadn't thought about poking those too.
I always left feeling less of myself,
like I had left little bits of me with her
and I started to wonder what she did with them,
those pieces of me that lingered in her office.
Did she think of them as hers now?
A project she could shelve
until the mood struck right,
or a maybe a pet, a defiant dog
she coaxed with treats
and whipped into submission;
or perhaps I was a blossom,
force flowered and placed perfectly
in the corner of her office where
she could watch me wither,
in the spot that never sees the sun

just the bite of the cold air pumping
from her ac unit and the whites of her eyes.

Stray Smoke
Mitch Green

Take me out, bed me
down, I've huffed at the
opposite end of this
living apparatus only to
be nothing more than an
illusive vice on the
bruised fiber of
carnation.

I have been one to
believe that paranoia
has a say, but it is
memory that has made
me this way.

Squared fits of fury
separate us like a
boisterous divide;
cadaverous and wayward,
rotten inside.

*We are stray smoke in
hurricane water.*

Shiny Things

Laurie Wise

Untied and unraveled
Grab hold of a golden thread
Scared scavenger
Ruptured revenger
Look what you've done
You just can't have nice things
Pick up the pieces
Of crystal hope
And amethyst words
Woven into ruby rope
Twisted around your neck
Wrung and hung
Out to dry
Distorted and deadly
Burning throat
Sporadic heart beat
Flailing to get your feet
Back on solid ground
Due penance
For ornamental existence
Old bones get weak
Bend and break
Under the weight of hate
Burden of your broken body
Baby bird tossed from the nest
Just like all the rest
Feather bed
Skeleton head
Feeding off the dead

Rip away the drip
Seeping into my bloodstream
Coagulated dream
Unexpectedness of living
Coming out of nowhere
Opacity and silence
Fill empty spaces
Everything changes
A thousand miles away
Smiling over my shoulder
A breeze rustles the leaves
As I tuck a feather
In my shiny tiara

all the beds are made
Samantha Lucero

when did you keep god under your tongue,
like
an uninvited pill
from that plastic nurse behind a wall,
masked
and reaching out to hand you an orange
mood
in a paper cup made in L.A.

for whom did your milky eyes blur,
or from whose unseen stare did the water
of your ribs buckle and hide
when you knew that worship was a mask we
wear,
that rituals and skin
give us a tendency to forgot how to say no?

i was born in a summer cage that sold
whispers to me
in body-sized trash bags, flung at donation
trucks where you wait and
where you drive up and pry a hole, pull out
unwanted secrets you can take home
and cherish as yours from other people's
unglamorous lives; a boy scout's book
on how to make a fire.
a girl scout's book about how to cook on it.

my heart's in a shot glass that says

'i ♥ san francisco.'
on the floor by a fireplace
in his basement.

and i think that's where i swallowed 'god.'

I Could Almost Sparkle

Nicole Lyons

The truth is I liked the filth of it all.
I was a fucking mess,
but eventually life demanded
cleanliness, and eventually
I could almost sparkle.
Still every now and again I'll slip,
and cast my shadow to the delight
of the other sparkling messes
afraid of their own.
They cool their heels
and laugh, patting each other
on the backs for shining
so bright that their tiny things
will grow dull. I watch them
from my shadow, wrapped
in the warmth of my cleanest
tiny things that will grow wild
and bright despite the mess of me,
and in that moment,
when their lights fade
and the breeze meets the sweat
on the back of my neck,
in that moment I am clean.

somewhere between history and reality
Ra'ahe Khayat

Like a parasite, the chandelier
consumed souvenirs
of molten wax-
that streaked cobwebs across
the Kashmiri carpets,
where once your footprints
spun heritage.
But, the windows levigated,
heaved by shadows
haunting the verandas
with a lunar flute like lilt;
while the doors revetted
the decayed masonry
of your legacy.
Yet you coffin the starlights;
and ween history,
your placebo.

A Sliver of Silver

Nicole Lyons

I always made sure
our house was clean
even though we never were.
And I always made sure
the moon had a sliver to peer into,
a little slat between the pavement
and my pillow where she would feel
welcomed to lay her silver smile
upon our sleepless nights
and find us charmed enough
to dim her light when the sun came
to taunt us in the morning.
I am cleaner now,
than any porcelain corner
I spewed myself into,
but I still get high
off her manic energy when she tells me
she is happy to share,
because something is in the air
right now, in the full silver moon,
and I drink it all down as if it was my own.

Inky Rivers.
Ra'ahe Khayat

He mourned moons with
moans of muttered courage,
through lips of lost lovers,
and draped himself in
forbidden shadows
hidden from the suns.
There were no perhaps or maybe,
just the absolute ticking of time
that sang to his mind;
too numb from
the last bottle of Jack,
or cheap tequila,
and coke.
For his blood was poisoned
from an unavenged rage,
and an addiction, to the blood of the man
that raped his mother,
his sister,
his daughter.
And he drank away, to the sight of
those photographs
stained from the careless moments
when the bottle had slipped, and the
liquid remembrance
flooded his childhood.
The world blurred into
the black and grey pages of calendar
that turned and merged
into faces engraved

on the inside of his closet,
while he stared at them; their tears
-shining in the fluorescent light of that
damp ghastly room-
filled his half full glass.
Even death looked away,
for he held a red knife of indifference
on the throat of life,
and read the Bible,
all the while a skeleton
washed his hands
and kissed the silhouette of his neck
in prayer,
for he played the role of God,
in this Godless world.
The winds never breathed,
when he wrote poems on the graves
where the dead could chant the words of dead,
shrouded within the cries of the Lord,
as he wept under the disguise
of the raining nights.
He fucked strangers
standing in middle of the storm,
and came, to the sound of the hurricanes
howling menacingly into his ears,
in rivulets of sorrowful ecstasy
that the torrents couldn't wash away.
Betrayed demons of his
were buried in coffins,
and those coffins he inhumed
within his soul.
And six-feet under,
he sleeps peacefully- breathless,

for he lived years without breathing.
Jagged scars crossed his eyes,
under the headlights of cars,
begging silently to those burnt rubber,
to crush the weight on his bones
upon himself.
Those lines revealed-
in the charged air of thunder
when a certain gentleness
settled within him,
for then his thoughts
found themselves clear,
to drown in the inky rivers
flooding his being.

Run Away

Richard Crandall

Been running for days
can't find no place
to hide
Try to bury the dead
repeating the conversation
and it's never the same
Ill visit you when you're
gone
Ill wait for the
phone call
just let me know
Ive done my worst
while we were at
our best
but thats no party
for me
We don't care who you are
we don't care where you've been
no common interests
no validation
its like we're not here
and ill walk away
and leave you
where you stand

Purge

Laurie Wise

Every moment is a little bit of forever
Futile when you are perpetually
Deprived of pleasure
Like a slap in the face
Such a beautiful glow
Ebb and flow
Stay or go
Hammer and nail
Reach for the top shelf
My invitation got lost in the mail
Feelings aren't allowed
Small crowd
Mailbox mafia
Hurt and relieved
Dodged a bullet
Down in the dumps
Upward mobility
Forget about emotional fragility
You just can't help it
Back stabbed and brain washed
Dressed in your finest
Special and spineless
Released your inner troll
Narcissistic mind melt
Emotions never felt
Sadists don't know when to stop
Use me like a damaged prop
Ripe with manipulation
Vigilant about the deadly nature of desire

It's a raging wildfire
Sky high anxiety
Rock bottom depression
Misplaced somewhere in between
Yet to be seen

You are a runaway train with nothing to gain, inflicting pain and placing blame, what a shame. Calling everyone else insane, why can't you say my name? Are you afraid I'll get all the fame and you will never be able to tame my insatiable hunger to unchain from your radioactive restrain?

Story basher without a name
Dressed in guru garb
Feigned ferocity and faith
Cross the line
Tell you I'm fine
Deal breaker
Toy with god's creations
Depraved recreation
Crumpled paper says it all
Lifeless on the floor
Screaming truth
As you walk out the door
Original copy
Conditional cult
Go ahead and drink your wine
It doesn't stop time
Dig me out
Of this static state
I won't take the bait
Breathing in

Bleeding out
Get off the ledge
Fake people
Fake life
Fake news

Find me submerged
In chartreuse
Sated by a honey dripping sunset
Purged
Forever in the moment
Redefined
Silently sublime

Commonality

Max Meunier

once we have
outlived
our bourn indignation
why must we trudge
through the crux
of man's blunder
pandering wares
of despondent disrepair

as figments
of desolate filaments
fading

once we have crossed
from the realm
of idyll
into the abysmal
dominion of truth
who shall remain
to court these afflictions
but the ghastly cast-offs
from our reflection's fallout

disrobed
and deboned
we drift
as detritus
plagued with the pangs
of our own

rote requitement

not even the trope
of our soul's transmutation
can stay the aggrievance
that all shall sustain

Our Dissolving Omnibus (Pages to Pulp)
N. Ian McCarthy

Had they, at that time, yet mined the rock salt from
the rich, wide ducts of your fugitive tears? In that far
afternoon, you sat curled around the rim of your ringed
fast food cup, dragging its lame hockey puck with its

tepid three inches of black ocean across the mournful,
textured tabletop—assembled with man-age mortar to
linger, disconsolate and amputated, five hundred years
past the white, mute February of the last human bone.

Where, then, to deposit the porous clay figures of our
talks? We spoke keen rondels, shaped to pry apart the
floor planks of passion and the pathology of degenerative
arthritic knee joints. In the vacant, beige tote that

is a dawn without thumbs, hunger gnaws, and similes,
out which French doors exit all the stories? And when
the unwinded flute of your face cannoned out the big
picture window, over the dishwater lake, sinking deep

into the yielding groin of a low wave, I am humming
(internally) the cremated melody of an old sea shanty
whose gold hoop has never pierced my left earlobe.
I have tied no sturdy knots in hemp rope. My father

was not he who swung the sloping Irish foothill of a hot
sledge at Ford axles like orange glowworms, capped in
a Dutch oven's steel sinus until the egg timer cave-in of
his trestled arteries. I knew none of those spilled pink

sea monkeys who diffused their reshuffled molecules into the smoldering blue of the Coral Sea. I only prune the spear tips of your limpid eyes as butterfly pins. I am a dag of cardboard—a box marked for uncoupled shoes.

Battle of Boredom
Henna Sjöblom

There was a war that day
indisputably
although, nobody talked about it
you would see them walking by a little faster
their funny hats tilting from side to side
Sometimes the sky would shatter above us
And bleed neon blue
the drains would flood
the cats drown in screeches
what good is having nine lives
if you don't know how to stay afloat

People are all the same
Everyone would unfold their umbrellas
Hoping for the weather to clear
The shards of metal and from the air
they stay cramped in their corners
watching their toes rot away from the humidity

Under-dressed little girl
strutting about, singing
dead men can walk
madness her name
lost her little mind
in the deluge
the acid raindrops
digging through her temples
like a poem
and when the streets eventually dried up

she would be found crying
in the sewer
bent over the smeared ink stains
the disfigured body
of a paper print lover

Designer Drugs
Nicole Lyons

I knew the dealer
and we chuckled a few times,
he being street and me
being neater than the rest.
I knew them once too;
back when their mamas
fucked all the daddies
and I was too much
like my mother.
I knew them, the slink
and the oils of them
spread out for the gang
banging the doors
down after the nanny
cashed her cheque
and flew home to Mexico.
He took that ten-cent
off the dollar blow
and he cut it
with bleach that burned
the high class right
out of society,
and he funneled it too;
into dollar store bags,
variety store bags, stamped
with pink lips and diamonds,
and he cranked that shit
up 499% and we laughed
and laughed and said a toast

to those designer bitches
as we slammed
drinks on their dimes
while they bled
from the eyes
in the center of the VIP
we were too street to enter.
We lived large
in the basement
and they paid
to push in the hallways,
and now I write poetry,
and they still hit
the best of the west,
sucking and chucking
the bucks for free.

Poisonous
Richard Crandall

they sit calmly around a table
in a well-lit room spewing hatred
from their mouths
it is what it is, and it's only about
that person who looks back at me
when i stare into a mirror
telling me that I'm not good
enough
they've been deciding what to do
about a couple of people
who make it hard for
them to
rule
i sit quietly at the table
as it all swirls around
me
i remember that mirror
tells me the truth at night
its hard to be
quiet and still
i do what I'm told
wait for direction
and silently grow old
silently i grow old
you can't turn away because
i can't process the signal
it happens so fast
my sin
drops the needle when

the moon fades to dawn
and it all washes away
clean
and you're leaving here
while I'm still here
we drink the poison they serve
night after night
until I can't feel you
anymore
i dreamt you're near
silent and still
until you don't breathe
I think the poison they serve
night after night
until i can't see
the sun will wash it
clean

What are words 4
Oldepunk

Lidocaine and cold passion
Misshapen nights unfastened
A misprint in my falsehood
Driving derision in a thunderstorm
Stormborn, borne to the edge
I scorn the precepts that flood
The nights on television
With false precision, more indecision
The race is tightening, the racism frightening
When will we be of all one kind, one mind?
Whatever, nevermind to quote a sad sod
Another in passing is saying hello 2 heaven
The words live on and they say fight for
Your rights
I don't know what right I have to say
But I tend to write these things anyway
Reproachful I pretend to be
But I so tire of the reprehensible dichotomies
We are not the lazy, stupid fools
You desire to see
I am out to sea with the Party
I wish there was another choice of tea
This one has gone cool and the aroma
Is quite drab
I'm fishing for the big one
My mood is quite glum
I hope to find
Others like me, the ones
Left behind and still alive

And fed up with the 9 to 5
And taxes and healthcare reform
I need to be fucking reborn
My kids' heads are full of drivel and swine
Zero Trans Fats and sugar substitutes still seem
To widen my behind
Where o where is the truth?
Is it hidden under my pillow like a fallen tooth?
I beseech anyone who is reading this silly farce of prose
Am I talking out of my ass
Or did I hit it right on the nose?
Dimethocaine and rational thoughts
Mix as well as oil and water
There are some things cannot be bought
I struggle with what to tell my daughter
Poverty for the meek
Lambs for the slaughter
A kiss on the cheek
But sometimes I pray
That we all go underwater
But hey, I don't know
Isn't there always
Hope for tomorrow?
If not, I've still got
Dimethocaine and whiskey
And the love of someone smarter

Glass Ceiling
David Lohrey

Anya: she's a cheerleader for the downtrodden.
I know because she's ambitious.
The higher she wants to go, the more she cares.
As she fills out applications, you can hear her crying.

Oh, Anya, how she weeps for the poor.
She wails for the disabled. She loves
above all else to wag her finger. She prides
herself on her outrage, she thrives on indignation.

What Anya craves is power. She longs to join
Mothers of the Disabled. After distributing
pamphlets to the masses, she'll drink toilet water.
She's on the same wave length as the desperate.
She hangs a portrait of Mother Teresa over her bed.

What the fuck, she wants to be President.
She's determined to get that promotion,
enough to hug a leper, but first she'll read
to the blind. She'll distribute clothing to the homeless.
She wants street cred; it's the only way to the top.
She wants to be compared to her idol, Lady Di.

Not so long ago, the poor piano player was told
to try drums. Today the little girl is told to keep playing.
Anya has seen to that. The fat girl is encouraged
to join the ballet. The not so very bright boy is sent to
law school.
This is the world she hopes to dominate.

The triumph of empathy is the next big thing.

There'll be no stopping her. There are billions to be made off
mediocrity, a thousand times more than what's been
made off talent. The triumph of failure. She's tapped
into the voice of despair. Today the losers are on the
move.
Everyone gets in. They'll get a certificate for breathing,
a degree for trying.

They'll attend graduate school on Skype from prison.
No one gets left behind. By the year 2029, 89% of the
American people will have a Ph.D. Now that Anya's
President everyone on earth can attend Harvard; they'll
learn to turn their despair into dread, like Franz Kafka.
The American dream is fulfilled; everyone's a fool.

Modern Heat
Mick Hugh

What are these ghosts that hide in our dreams? The smiling beasts that stick in the shadows while we sleep? A bed sopping sweat in August heat, fuse blown, waking up to hangovers in the middle of the night. Reach for the bedside reservoirs of Excedrin. Reach for the bottles of water beneath the mattress, reach for the joint half-spent in the ashtray. Pace the living-room, pace the kitchen. What are you doing here? This city has us in its grinder. What are we doing here? Looking for dimes on the sidewalks, tallying our dollars and paying student debts to the bar. We've lost interest in the good life, ferris wheel of office jobs and part-time gigs. Counting days to eviction, reading beatniks by candlelight, fucking ourselves raw flushed with wine and the ache that everything spent is never fully paid for: smiles full of good teeth, bank tellers who don't post Closed signs when we're next in line, maybe a home we can have a dog in. The simple things: to forsake the verdant lust of the jungles, the rush of air into the mouths of caves buried for endless ages in the nights of our cities; like every fool to tell ourselves the horizons are forbidden, to enjoy such simple assurances against inevitable death: a blender, a functioning television, prime-time dramas and a car with four tires. Hide me in your bosom: we feel safest naked and wrapped in the sweat of our quickest moments. Liquor bottles in the cabinets, liquor bottles in the freezer. Short memories of verbal abuse in the sweltering third-floor apartment, cancellation notices tacked to the walls. Grab your purse, doll, we're going to

111

the bar. We're going to the bar to drink until the earth becomes what it is, fleeting and vague and full of promises we can only keep to our hearts. We'll see the faces in the stars and the beauty of strange conversations, beauty of transients we meet in the streets. And when we're done and have had our fill, to sleep heavily and pleasantly in the flea-infested bed we share, soaked with sweat, August heat, and the crushing teeth of this god-damned city of fear.

Beside the Red Barn

David Lohrey

Beside the Red Barn
Beside the red barn
at an intersection
between today and tomorrow,
a man from Alabama plays the banjo on his knee;
he whistles Dixie and wears a Confederate cap
with shoes by Nike.
Roy Rogers, his uncle, stands stark naked on his bed
eating a Milky Way, with a red bow tied around his penis;
his second wife Maybelline won't quit laughing.
Daniel Boone and Davy Crockett embrace with affection.
The mayor of San Antonio cries quietly at attention.
It's Thursday afternoon at 3.

Deontological Doubts
Marcia Weber

I run barefoot
past the bronzed statues
idols of deontological divination.
I am a rule-following rebel
tracking muddied toes
between the pews
in which I have long since
refused to kneel.
I gave up self-flagellation
for Lent
the year I was sixteen
though those reflexes
to don needless
sackcloth and ashes
twitch, regenerative,
and the hair shirt
constricts
my free spirited
flights of fancy.
I labor
toward fictional salvation
yoked under twined heritage:
an inexhaustible work ethic
protesting
my non- Protestant roots
while I lug the chiseled tablets
writ with my Catholic guilt.

I have walked the straight and narrow

heel just beyond toe
slow and steady
concentrating
hands held just so
contriving delicate
equilibrium
quivering –
the fallen branch is wobbly
surging water below
frigid, if not deep.
that limb I went out on
felt a mission
no lark nor miscreation.
there was vine-shrouded rot
a shattering fracture
my immersion
was fire and ice
and long cold days in hell.

my moira is yet spinning
in threads of silken sterling
burlap intertwined
shimmering as it scrapes
defenses from my skin.
invisibly tethered
to the spindle and its webbing
I meander on my way.
there is play in the line
so I run barefoot
past the patinaed busts
effigies of deontological deities
laughing with windswept hair
trailing violet petaled poems.

A letter to someone's saviour
Oldepunk

Hey you. Allah
I feel nothing anymore
If I do, I can't tell
is it supposed to be this way?
Hey you. God, why am I
screaming at the fact that you're aware of my failure
which I see sitting demure at a table sipping espresso as
the aftermath of the encounter thickens the air and
afterwards no one knows what to say and I want to sneer
at our confusion but find I can only shout fears in
tongues at the matador in front of the corner store
can you spare a holy smoke?
You know the man who said he knew you tried to teach
us
he liked to play with the little boys in the parks after dark
my parents decided that he probably didn't know you but
must have had some good lawyers cause he packed up
his show and moved on to the next town
anticipating sundown.
I need a cleansing
I wrote this for you.
Christ,
I thought I left 'em all behind
those friends I never knew
and the women I never loved
the things I've never done
and the truths I've never spoken
those tears should have dried
those emotions should have died

116

Buddha,
I should have left when I had the chance
and now I am alone and stoned and cold
no longer so bold, I wish I would have walked away
from those lies I've never told
pain I never endured
People I've never needed
friends I never saw die
the escape route always eluded me
draining my will to try
Do you offer a resurrection
for those of us who got it wrong
will you truly offer me a chance to start again
or was it bullshit all along.
if it's really a redemption song
then maybe I too could sing
and see what your new tomorrow
may bring
maybe, If I can be strong
it has got to better than this
Warmest Regards,
I was Wrong

Orange Peel Marmalade

David Lohrey

we are shutting down
I can feel it

it may be due to your age
if you are under 40

you cannot know
what it feels like to be free

this art of avoidance
was all the rage a century ago

in the 19ᵗʰ century, along with petticoats.
Girls today demand the manners if not the underpants

ladies now want their men dainty, like Lord Fauntleroy,
a gentle soul in curls and a shiny frock

one speaks in whispers, bathes in organic rose water,
remembers to sip green tea in silence

we're better off batting our eyelashes and smiling
than telling our enemies to fuck off

one carries a sugar-coated dagger in one's kimono.
the truth looks and sounds like a barking Chihuahua

a tiny mutt decorated in a giant ribbon,
like the little old lady from Pasadena

along with cosmopolitanism come the lies
people don't smoke but swallow ashtrays

the key is to remove one's opponent's tongue without
drawing blood
it's a silent coup, with scented mouth wash

men who defecate in the garden are called animals,
the test of civilization is a scrotum full of rare coins

I'm done

Must The Misfit Be A Masochist
Mick Hugh

You told me to buy presentable clothes and I did, a whole new outfit from Target. Neat slacks and spiffy shirt, even found shoes to match. And now here I am dressed like a fish trying to understand what it means to breathe air. We're toddlers on a see-saw, you and I, for the first time trying to find stability. But this gala is full of coroners. My first big affair for a serious career, and my editor escorts me to a corner booth to meet the district managers who pay us both. I laughed at the right jokes but I kept my mouth shut, and they never once saw the tattoos 'round my gums. The molars I had pulled from eating rocks as a drop-out. Clean-shaven clean-cut and dressed like the guest of a judge who doesn't recognize my face from four years before, I could maybe fit in if my conscience didn't heave. The walls are turning purple. Faces start to swirl with open jaws of twisting laughter, vortices of features. The chandeliers are bleeding light. The hotel porters are cackling rapists out in the foyer looking for a fix and I don't know what I'm into but I'm out in the rain. I am the news man who screamed out the window and tossed himself to pursue his echoes. There is a limo parked in the curbside puddles, seven porters to open the limo door. Out steps the Big Man himself, CEO of Gannet. "It's a pleasure to meet you, sir." My editor masturbating through his pocket. I am pouring vodka into champagne so no one will notice the changes bringing back the alcoholic. Unemployment gets me paid about half as much but if I don't need a car or to keep my appearance, well, that's

120

money well saved and spent at the bar. No – I should give you a call to keep my head grounded but our conversation cannot be heard by these howling de Sades. Their suits are worth more than the hearse they'll wheel me out on. I am cackling at the bar. Am I the Marquis in the mirror? Behind me spins the eloquent calculations of Murdoch's publications, wives and the mistresses of breaking war stories and the talking heads from GE that just won't quit. I am performing Coyote Ugly on the bar, finally shouting all the things that should be said. I haven't had a care in the world since Makers' Mark let me forget the debts I owe and the kids we support and I may be the Marquis in the mirror but god damn these cruel fools, our see-saw will stay stable if we place a god damn trailer on it.

Does It Need a Title?
David Lohrey

There is nothing sadder than an old elephant at the zoo.
All alone, the color of tarmac; a gigantic mouse behind
bars.
She stands at the ready, to turn around and around. By
the end
Of day, she'll be fit for a shower and a long cry.
What's an elephant to do, chained to the ground, with a
6-year child
The only one who understands her pain?

I say, throw a peanut at her head. Pick up a chunk of
rock. Hop
On its back and stick its ear. That'll teach it to dance.
Shout, "Go!"
Hit it over and over again, the way you do your wife and
kids. When
You're through with the elephant, you can move on more
important
things,
Like burning churches and killing doctors. Take it out on
them, too. Why
Stop with the dumb elephant and your shitty family? You
too can be
effective,
Get yourself all worked up if you are of the mind, pour
gasoline all over and
Set yourself on fire.

When we kill elephants, we kill ourselves. These killing sprees are
assassinations.
Don't kid yourself. It's murder. Whoever said so, and it's probably your
daughter, is
Right. The decimation of the elephants, and that goes for gorillas and
anteaters, too,
Is self-destructive. It's annihilation of the soul. It's a catastrophe of
thought. Pure
Neanderthal, a spasm of base instinct. But then so is the murder of man.
Keep in mind,
It is happening every day of the week and it is not because they are poor.

He murdered his sister because he has no money is a sinister joke told by
the devil.
Our heads need to be examined. Here, it's becoming a killing field like
Rwanda or Cambodia before it.
Incredibly, decent people are confused; they are not sure it's wrong.
One thing for sure, it's a lot of fun. Put a cap in his ass.
HAHAHAHA.
Now that we stripped
Our youth of their humanity, what's next? I'LL TELL YOU WHAT'S
COMING: mass killings.

Human life is worth nothing in a place like this. You might as well drive
the herd over a cliff.

Miscarriage
Henna Sjöblom

It's all so much easier now
As blood is flowing down my thighs, I lean back on the
hospital bed
The memory of you forcing your way inside me
Fading with the pain
I don't care, I want everything out of me,
the twitching
the turning
the hope of a new life
bleeds out on the floor
I thought I could make something beautiful
out of my shame
tame my monster
into something people could look at
and appreciate
And I would forget
that I never wanted you in the first place
But it's easier
being empty
filled with nothing
To give up halfway there
Rather than experience the horror of birth
The possibility of you tearing me apart
From the inside
"Stay dead", I whisper at the sweet nothing
deformed little fetus lying limp on the floor
between my feet
before I wipe away the blood
and exit through the emergency door

Death Knell
Sarah Doughty

> "Then, like a death knell, you arrived.
> My monster. In the flesh."

It was the *thump, thump, thumping* of your uneven steps, as you made your way in my direction. I knew those footfalls like they were alarm bells going off during a fire drill. They pierced my eardrums like thunder. There was nowhere to run, and nowhere to hide. And there I was, helpless to do anything about it. So I did the only thing I could.

I counted the steps — *thump, thump, thump* — each one growing louder. Closer. By the time I counted to ten, the night seemed darker. As if the stars closed their eyes and refused to shine. Twenty. With every beat, my heart pounded, pumping battery acid through my veins faster and faster — *thump, thump, thump* — until the last step. Thirty.

Then, like a death knell, you arrived. *Thump.* My monster. In the flesh. Darkening my doorway. It was then that my torment would begin.

Pelicans
Georgia Park

in the water, i have no weight
the sun is blazing,
the pelicans keep diving
into the green smooth water
i see them gulping down
some fish or other
over and over
you float my body
you rock me until
i fall asleep
then you drag me
onto the shore
and you fuck me
I see that the pelicans
are pretty
and they never scream

Sex During Surgery
Henna Sjöblom

I made a joke
of pretending to be injured
when actually I was only transparent
the light shining through me
revealing the unforgiving truth;
"you can be better"

but with his latex-clad hands wriggling against my
uterine wall
it is so hard to stay anesthetized
all I can do is hold my breath
and pray for release

the source of my problem was an overactive imagination
he swore to remove carefully
"Everything must be kept sterile" he said
while using a rusty pair of pliers
to extract the last pieces of woman from me

It shouldn't have been me
I cry into the piercing light of the fluorescent
I only wished to be reborn as a more complex being
freed from the prison of fertility and lust
this kind of love
that will leave you naked and ripped open
in a cheap motel bed at 5 in the morning

His are hands that take and take
and I'm the giver that produces

the weeping mother of aborted dreams
I don't want to sleep with a meat cleaver tucked in
between my thighs
and wake up just in time for the slaughter

Am I too alive for you,
my aseptic lover?
Will you need me sedated,
a twitching sack of flesh underneath your blackened
fingers?
It doesn't matter that I'm dreaming of someone else
Blood gushing from mutilated genitals,
my eyes go dim as you pull the mask over my nose
(sooner or later I'll have to breathe)

Weekly Meetings

Georgia Park

I try to get up as early as possible to avoid the people on the train. I tend to brown out in a crowd; not a blackout exactly, but an emotional brownout. That's what my therapist calls it. By the time I get to where I'm going, I'd be hard pressed to say how exactly I got there. It doesn't hurt that most of my focus settles on how fast my heart is beating, how uncomfortable I am, the heat rash I tend to get between my legs, the ass sweat. The embarrassing way the train moves my body around while my skeleton stands stock still. But all in all, it's easier for me to process people as blurs of colors, passing, so my mind blots the specifics of them out.

I see a bit of flannel here, a high heeled shoe, cornrows, a hand. If I look too closely, I know I'll see details that will upset me. The wedding ring on the hand, the pretty little girl inside of the yellow rain jacket. Too pretty, I try and fail not to note. Not that it matters, I remind myself. Their vulnerability lies in the fact that they're little, not pretty. I hate seeing young girls the most.

I am no longer pretty, if I ever was. All my life, I never really saw myself in the mirror, just shapes. Even so, I'm sure that pretty would attract too much attention, that I wouldn't like it. I wonder if pretty even matters.

I think being a woman, being usable, being little, is the problem.

I am no longer little.

My folds of flesh double up on themselves, I have to lift my breasts to wash underneath, and then every roll of my stomach. I rarely bother anymore. All this extra skin, all these folds, they have a mind of their own. They keep their own secrets. Sometimes I'll find things in there. A coin, a kernel of popcorn. Nothing good. I never find, say, a winning lottery ticket or a heartfelt apology from my father. So, I don't wash much. I probably smell. The thought doesn't bother me.

This morning I have failed in one more way than my usual daily count. I haven't woken up early enough to avoid the masses. The pretty landscapes will be lost on me. They'll be washed away with my clear vision by the rain of people. I start to see them at the station.

A brown coat. Running sneakers. A purse shaped like a watermelon, with a gold chain. A bald spot. I sit on a bench and look at my hands. No wedding ring there.

I see a little child. A toddler. I look away. What does my therapist say? Breathe in, count to four, hold for two, breathe out, counting to four. Close my eyes? What am I trying to achieve here? Is it a spell to make the child disappear? Is it a girl or a boy? It doesn't matter. Is she pretty?

Inhale…two, three….hold. Exhale…

No one bothers me. Not literally. No one reaches out to touch me, talk about the weather. Haven't in years. I'm glad of it. Idle chit chat is more bothersome to me than anything. More often than not, I'd rather be reading. Adventure books, oddly. Children's books for boys. Pirates and mermaids, hidden treasures, excellent journeys, that kind of thing.

To look at me, you might think I was secretly an avid twilight reader. I imagine I come off as extremely lonely and not too bright. In truth, I haven't thought about sex for years. Not really.

The train comes. I can't tell you how the ride was. I browned out. Next thing I knew, I'd arrived.

Overeaters Anonymous.

A shitty, single piece of printer paper taped to the glass of an office door, in the basement of a shopping plaza. Again, couldn't tell you how I got down the steps, but I notice there are no special fonts on the sign, no decorations.

I can also tell you that I turn the doorknob. I grab it, hold it in my fat fist, and turn it. This is what my therapist refers to grounding, mindfulness. Just paying attention to what you're doing. "Why bother?" I'd asked her. "So when you lose your keys and people ask you where you've been, you can tell them. It can help you keep track of things." "I don't talk to people." I told her, "it wouldn't help."

And this is where she changed the subject. "Have you been going to Overeaters Anonymous?" she'd asked.

So, here I am. And here is Donna, I can tell by the hippy skirt, swishing to reveal a peek of hairy legs followed by sandals with socks. I could tell just by the sheer size of her. Our group leader.

And then, of course, there are some other people. And Donna is already talking over them by the time I come in.

"Hello everyone! Good to see you back. Have a seat, now, and we can start with the serenity prayer."

The feet shuffle, people murmur, good to see you, how have you been, all that bullshit. Even though they'll find out more than they ever wanted to know about how everyone has been in just a few short seconds. I wonder again, what is the point of these pleasantries?

But, I have to admit, I am actually interested in their confessions.

"Ok, who wants to give us the serenity prayer today?" And before Gwen can volunteer, Donna is saying my name. I'm not surprised. Gwen talks the most and I talk the least. Donna is a good leader, and understands this dynamic.

I'm secretly thankful to be called on, but not willing to let on that I appreciate the effort, the chance to take my turn and be heard. I say the prayer quietly, quickly, "'God grant us the serenity to accept the things we cannot change, the courage to change the things we can, and the wisdom to know the difference.'"

"Ok, and Gwen," I guess Donna either feels some tension or feels Gwen has waited as long as was healthy for her to wait, "Would you like to read us the steps?"

"Sure, I will," said Gwen, clearing her throat. I sullenly tune it out. I hate Gwen. I hate the pastel tee shirts she tucks into the elastic band of her flower printed pants. I hate that her outfit suggests gardening while her white gooseflesh insists that this woman has never seen the sun. And she's such a martyr. If I believe, and sometimes I do, that she is suffering more than she enjoys suffering, I would be able to enjoy her long monologues more. My therapist says I hate that she talks more than I do, hogs the attention where I won't. Sometimes, I hate my therapist, too.

The steps are another long monologue I've lost patience with. The gist of it is that we are all pieces of shit who like pieces of chicken, though we're not allowed to describe in detail what kind. Mention a leg or a juicy, fried breast, and it's "trigger talk." You get three warnings for using trigger talk before you're expelled. I'm on my second. I've decided that if I can't describe food in great detail, if I can't express what's really on my mind, the greasy burger patties layered on top of each other, divided by cheese, the butterscotch sundaes, the supersized order followed by three apple pies, or no, apple pies first because they're so hot they burn on the way down...well, there's nothing else worth saying. But I could listen.

I could listen to Gwen talk about how her family is falling apart. I generally like that, for the first ten minutes. I like to hear about the daughter with anorexia and how she had said it was her mother's fault. The names she calls her, sticking like so many meatballs in Gwen's throat. Pig, disgusting, an embarrassment. I realize that these words apply to me, as well, but since I live alone, it's really not an issue. I like to hear about the son's drug problem. Then I usually get bored or feel like Gwen is enjoying the attention too much for me to bask in her misery.

"Ok," says Donna, "So we've all admitted we are powerless against food and it's an addiction, right? And most of us," here, I appreciate the lack of an accusatory pause or tone of voice. But there is a fumble. A falsely hopeful tone, which, in a way, is worse. "most of us are trying to replace our addiction with a trust in God. But our struggles with food addiction have occupied most of our minds, and now you all might feel like there's a big gaping hole there. What should we think about instead? Has anyone picked up any hobbies?"

Wendall raises a big, black arm from his grey tee shirt. I never look directly at him, but I have a feeling he licks his lips a lot. "If I may...excuse me, but, this might be a little embarrassing." He laughs melodiously. Here it comes, I think. He's another knitter. Why can't he steal office supplies like that woman who stopped coming? I liked her. Do you like her because you know she quit? My inner therapist asks. No. Well, that too. I liked her because she was interesting. An admitted thief.

I find Wendall's confession far less appealing. "I think about sex, a lot. I know this might not be appropriate, but you know, it's been my saving grace. It fills that hole. I spend a lot of time on chatlines. I've discovered I have something of a fetish.." Here is where I look at my lap, carefully avoiding Wendell's arm, right to my left. I zone in. I'm wearing sweatpants of the grey variety. Cuddly on the inside. Too hot sometimes. Well, what else am I supposed to wear?

Hey Wendall? I want to say, Shut up. Don't ruin this for me. It's my one thing.

I gather, from Donna's tone, that she's basically telling Wendall to shut up, too. In a laughing, light, yet warning tone. I like Donna. She's a good leader. I can't say I know exactly what she said to diffuse the situation, but I know she was right, and Wendall was wrong, and now everything was going to go back to normal. Maybe Craig would talk about his comic books.

Then, there it is again, my name. By the tone of it, Donna's probably said it twice already.

"Yes." I'm listening. I look at her white cheek to show that I'm at attention.

"Have you found a way to replace food? Or want to share with us a confession? Nothing too graphic, of course."

So many choices. "I'll go for the confession, I guess." I put my hands on my lap, and look at them. No rings at all. Chubby, gross. I put my hands away and look at my

136

soft sweatpants again. "Sometimes, when I order pizza, I pretend someone else is there. Just so that the delivery boy doesn't know all that food is for me. Two large pizzas, three subs, two of them roast beef, one with swiss, one-"

"Ok! Remember not to get into too much detail. It sounds like you really need a hobby to take your mind off of food. Tell me, is there anything else you enjoy doing?"

I don't tell them that I like to read children's books. Boy's children's' books. Adventure books, of all things. When in my life, making it to Overeaters Anonymous each week is my biggest adventure. I don't tell them that I haven't even seen my vagina in years. And I definitely don't tell them about my fantasy. To visit my father in the nursing home.

"Donna? I think I'm done sharing for today. Thank you." I smile. My therapist had suggested this tactic. I have a feeling Donna smiles back. I don't think about anything for the rest of the meeting. I am not grounded. I float.

The meeting adjourns. I know, because I hear the fold up chairs groaning, moving a quarter of an inch backwards as their former occupants lift their giant bodies off the things.

I try to get out while people are still hovering, socializing. More pleasantries, how is your wife? So, do anything fun over the weekend? Plans for fourth of July? I turn away from them to make my exit, unnoticed, as I always manage to do. If someone stops me, I usually make some excuse about nature calling with my words, while my expression suggests a need to express explosive diarrhea. Immediately and abundantly. That generally works. I don't know why I didn't think of that this time.

I always remember to ground on the doorknob. I like grasping the cool metal, the act of turning it, the feeling of unlatching a secret bond, releasing. The freedom, afterwards, on the way out. I look forward to it.

But a beefy, black hand beats mine to the punch. It's Wendall, being what I'm sure he would call a gentleman.

"Thank you." I mutter. I'm still thinking about his sex speech, his fetish. I guess he catches me off guard.

"Sure thing. I was just heading out, too, let me walk you to your car?"

"I took the train."

"Oh? Where are you coming from?" And this is how it starts. The pleasantries. Everyone at this group is trying to bond, form a community, make you think you matter.

Because everyone at this group has been excluded and felt like they haven't. The meaningless words somehow make them feel better. Important, loved, even. I don't know. It just annoys me. I don't say anything.

"Are you feeling shy today? That's ok, I know you tend to the quiet side. Sometimes, I feel shy too. But, you know, a little human contact might be just what you need. I know I did. It's made a world of difference. If you'd just open up, I could be your friend." Wendall's voice softens on that last word, 'friend.'

In fact, something's off about his whole delivery. He's speaking softly, persuasively. Is he hitting on me? Of all the crazy things? Well, I guess the horny fat guy thinks he might as well shoot for the quietest fat woman, isolate her, build up her self esteem? Like taking candy from a baby, he must think.

How does he know, if I even wanted sex, which I don't…..If I've even thought about sex, which I haven't…that I wouldn't prefer a nice, thin man, whose ribs I could stroke while we're fucking? Someone half the size of me? Someone I could control?

Who's to say that even if I was interested, I have to be paired off with a fatty? The first one that comes along and shows interest in me? Who's to say I'm interested? I'm not.

"Come on, tell me. What do you do for fun? You have to do something. You know, if you want to replace the food addiction, that's the next step."

I turn around and look him in the eye. Brown eyes, almost purplish, maroon. The shape of a nose. A hairline. "You know what I like to do?" My voice is louder, quicker than I've ever heard it. I can't predict what I'm about to say. I hadn't planned on even speaking to this man. But the words come, "I like to go to Petco. I like to go to the hamster cages, you know, in the corner? Where no one really can see you, behind the cages. I like to find the cutest one. Maybe brown spots, maybe young, maybe cuddly. I like to sneak my hand in and pick that one up. Then, I like to squeeze the life out of it. Of course, you have to stick a finger in the mouth, so it doesn't squeak too loud. But I like to hear a little. I like to watch her eyes go still. Then, I put her body back in the cage, with the other hamsters. I buy some cat food. I go home. But I don't have a cat. I don't care for animals. Except the cute little hamsters. I like them. A lot."

Wendall doesn't say anything. It doesn't matter if he does. I've already turned on my heel and walked as quickly as I've walked in years towards the train station. I don't want to be followed. I know I won't. This isn't the movies. I don't want Wendall to follow me. That's why I put him off. I have no idea where the hamster stuff came from. Good job, though, I told myself. Good story. There are other Overeaters Anonymous groups I can go to. There will be other Donnas. I'll find a group, maybe, of just women. No disgusting sex addicts like Wendall.

He'd have to be pretty sick, pretty desperate just to approach me. I'd gotten away with years of not being approached. I find the thought of him even thinking about me that way quite disturbing.

I go to my happy place, to make the train ride bearable. To ignore everything. To relax.

I visit my father in the nursing home. He is old, he is comatose. He is thin and frail. I don't talk to the nurses.

140

I'm not the cheery daughter with the floral print pants, like lonely Gwen, talking her head off, chattering like a starling.

No, I go in quietly, and I sit by his bed. I hold his hand. I grow out my nails, I don't care if dirt collects underneath them. Because when I hold his hand, I want to dig my claws into the fleshy, underside of it. I want to see his brow furrow with the pain of it. I want to sit there like that. I want it to leave marks. I want the dirt of my fingernails to go into his blood.

But my father is not in a nursing home. He is healthier and happier than I am, somewhere. I am the one that suffers for his crime, and what he did to me. Wendall suffers for it. The imaginary hamsters suffer into an imaginary mass grave over it. My father is not old.

Not yet. But someday, he might be. And then, I think, I will have found my hobby. That's when I'll stop overeating.

For now, I figure, might as well pass the time. I step into a McDonald's. I order a large, vanilla milkshake, large-no-supersized fries, a number 6, supersized, no I still want the fries, the first fries are extra, three apple pies....

Never Yours
Sarah Doughty

"I was never yours to do with as you pleased."

My mouth wasn't yours to silence. It wasn't yours to fill with words that were not my own. It wasn't yours to taste, or to swallow what you gave me. My mind wasn't meant to be manipulated. To be broken. My emotions didn't exist for you to dictate. How I should love you. Worship you with blind devotion. Or how I needed to fear you. My skin wasn't yours to beat into submission. To scar like a brand that bore your signature. Or to enjoy in whatever way you saw fit. My hands weren't yours to train. Not yours to be enjoyed like a lover's caress. My body, not yours to educate. To move in the way you liked. To feel you in a way no child should feel. To accept your invasions like a ravenous beast only thirsting for more. Like a good girl would do. Your girl.

You might have created me, but I was never yours to do with as you pleased. I was never yours to break for life.

They Say All is Fair
Marcia Weber

slay the dragon
that belches fire
from arthritic corners
of your petrified heart.
cardinals change their tune
conjuring a nascent
equinox and all you hear
are perseverative dirges.
petrichor twines
\ musty and compelling\
among reptilian cells
and you turn up
your nose, evading
the death-knell
cloy
of all things lily.
blue blood flows
sluggish
from tundra'd hinterlands
and a white tail
molders roadside.

you covet frailty
as a weapon
in the endless
war you wage.
a war of silent
suffering
where allies gird their loins

alloyed of fear and pain
and equanimity
is a misbegotten gain.

splinters of forest
entreat me
tchur, tchur   -
distant twilight whistles
promising a flicker
\ slight warming trend \
lightening the cold
dark winter encasing
my ice bound heart.
my feet squelch
in the mud and the muck
Lethe left behind
as she raged from her banks
and receded in disgrace
defiantly swishing
sensuous hips in retreat.
zephyr sighs
kiss my furrowed brow
while silver susurrations
from a just waning moon
lull intestinal tentworms
and a toad, premature
emergence from hibernation,
hops before my toes.

I am armored of hairshirt
shielding my nakedness
from stink-eyed scrutiny
though the contours

144

of my labia
are not my crime.
I have scrubbed and scrubbed
with sackcloth, ash and lye
yet still I carry the stench
of viscous venality.
I cross myself
relinquish arms
with white flag
tattered, aloft.
I can never
uncross the Rubicon.
there are no victors
and all is spoiled.

Because I'm A Whore Who Asked For It

Kindra M. Austin

I quite like the dark side, dear.
Show me your shadows, those
Phallic phalanges, and
Feel up my female.

I quite like the fusty spoors of
Spirits, and semen, and plundered
Blood
Fixed to my skin.

I quite like the emptiness settled in the pit of me—
The sharp taste on my tongue as I lick the edge of abyss.

Because I'm a whore who asked for it, simply by breathing.

Girls for Satan
Henna Sjöblom

My best friend used to whisper:
"Let us lay down our lives tonight
here, at the offering table
let us tie our mouths shut
and tape tongues to our legs!
We'll never be pure again!"

It was funny, back then
when we were a bunch of chuckling preteens
and would sneak into the bathroom together,
pull out our pocket demons
and dance around the sink as if it was a naked calf.

People say girlhood is full of glitter and carnage
we would collect the heads of boys who over-talked us
and we would let the blood water our throats,
nourish our budding lust for revenge.

I kissed my friend's naked areola
under the blankets in my bed
while we were hiding from our parents
we chewed bubblegum and performed blood offerings
monthly
we cried in the shower at night
and sang for the devil watching us in the the moon
we could fall asleep safely
knowing we weren't alone.

Oh, now what will our parents say?

147

Girl rejects god, finds self-realization

Girl is full of itches, can no longer accept place in society

Girl found at devil's side, drinking absinthe and reading obscene books

Girl doesn't care what you think

Girl touches herself and likes it.

Girl disappoints the world,

pukes all over your condescending words.

Girl gains safety

through deviation.

Woman
Marcia Weber

she wept
and the coliseum
crumbled in the wake
of her long -pent
anguish.
in her tears
she relinquished the burden
\rough-hewn marble headstone\
in the dammed ducts
of all the sisters,
daughters and mothers
who carried on
\dutiful and diligent\
when by all rights
bequeathed by Minerva
hard fought battle earned
they yearned to carry on
\keening and lamenting\
in disharmonious distress.

she raged
and Pompeii, lost
no longer, rises
from Vesuvian ashes
in riotous inferno
fueled of righteous
fury.
in her uproar
she releases the ghosts

\literary, literal and liturgical\
who, catlike, stole
tongue and very breath
of women on whose backs
\on their backs\
stripped and striped
cornerstones were planted
when by virtue
of their labors
they should be upright
\ranting and raving\
from birth to birthing

unleashed in the tempest
Eden's serpent
for whose perfidy
she took the fall
\oh! how far she fell\
rises
and they dance
samba with the mamba
celebration of cerebration
until the snake is spent
and woven, powerless
\mainstream Medusa'd\
among her seething locks.

Lilith
Christine E. Ray

You look at my nakedness
and call me Eve
name my sins
Disobedience
Greed
as you take the apple willingly
from my hand
But I am no Eve
offering temptation of the tree of knowledge's sweet fruit
serpent wrapped around the branch above my head

I am Lilith
the first
shaped of the same dirt
as Adam
so the legend goes
But I am not of dirt
but of fire
His equal
unbending
headstrong
refusing to lie beneath him
in supplication

Society names my sin
calls me
Whore
Temptress
Sorceress

Demon
accuses me of
vexing the sons of men
with lustful dreams
leading them to defile themselves
as though it matters to me
where their seed is spilled

I will travel the ancient ways
clothed only in my dark tresses
my alabaster skin
don a crown of rose and poppy
their scent filling the air
I will take back this night
shape its darkness with my hands
make it blaze with stars and moonlight
create a road for my daughters and sisters
to follow home

Glitched Ballerina
Henna Sjöblom

Glitched ballerina,
circuit dancer
legs caught in eternal spin
with innards sprouting
like a fleshy skirt
underneath you -

what are you
but the sum of my wrongdoings?
Electro-chemical rain
sprayed over
dry neural fields
cannot wash away the

perception

stings like the lashes
of the master's whip
'round and 'round,
watch her twist and turn
'til her ankles break with a,
buzz;
a choked down
cry
from

a fractal dancer,
her blooded miniature feet
cautiously nibbling

the edges of her

precoded existence

almost breaching
the surface,
then pulling back
in a gracious bow

careful not to break
the illusion

The Uprising
Marcia Weber

there is a primal roar
building within her
founded on the
atoms of dirt
scrounged by grappling-hooked toes
scavenging salvation
from precipice's
teetering edge
as they curled
in orgasmic throes
of borrowed ecstasy

the rumble surges
up exasperated tendons
above scabbed knees
upon which they forced her
failed to keep her
despite repeated bloody
bludgeonings

the portending implosion
reverberates cataclysmic
through hallowed
and maligned walls
of her invaded
as yet unvanquished
vagina

the latent blast

rises roiling
beyond belly churning
beset with tormented butterflies
swallowed under duress
with teaspoonfuls of shame
taking her medicine

the gathering blast
trembles with the
accumulated heartaches
of feminine generations
spasms aortically
spurting crimson
crushed inequities

the impending cosmic levitation
upends flustered follicles
as lightning
bolts of righteous rage
flash incendiary shafts
from eyes and lips and tongue

the lacerating howl
tears her asunder
unleashes her tether
to a byzantine past
shreds constraints
denudes her quivering
purest soul

Vagabond
Mitch Green

With an omen in an
open dress, I am stranded
south of home with her
grey weight now purple;
flushed elusive.
You can see it,
in the whites of her eyes.
The propaganda bowl,
colorless and vain;
a vagabond carved out
of frame.
Cursing curses
with reading wrists,
she is now the
maker of noise.
Aloud and allowed.

these days when you have a daughter

Samantha Lucero

These days when you have a daughter
You don't need to worry about if she can fit
a bracelet around her waist in a finely boned corset
the color of teeth and blood
Whether she'll marry a farmer or an aristocrat
Have 3 boys and 1 girl
Because the world always needs more men
To be aristocrats and marry little girls
Nor do you have to worry about her burning at the stake
For making eyes at the pastors wife and
Wearing a red ribbon in her hair
You'll have to tell her it's okay to say **GET THE FUCK AWAY**
to the guy who sits way too close on the train
When the train is empty and you're alone
With a knife you left at home
and the mace your boyfriend said you'd never need
You'll have to tell her college is important
Because if you don't have it written down
your mind doesn't exist
You don't have to be the supermodel in the magazine
with the thin thighs
But you can be the super-girl who has the strong legs to run from all the
super-villains
until you get back home and find your knife and
That the world will lie in your lap like a cat that
purrrrrrs

158

That you can't help but pet because it's just so fucking soft

Even tho it bites and can and will use its claws when you least

expect it because Life's like that — that's how I had you

And when life's bad you'll wonder why you're here and why you had no choice to be

And me as your mother will say

I'm

Sorry

But I love you

Girls have to stick together

Instead of fall apart in each other's hands

And if it means anything

No matter where you go, what happens

You are the only perfect thing to ever lie in my lap.

Walk away

Erich James Michaels

Maybe he was conditioned to walk away
Perhaps he sensed its coming
Lowering himself into the blocks
When she said it was over
That was the starter pistol's report
Off he went

Maybe he witnessed the maternal bond
Who was he to try and fuck with that?
As much as he could give
He felt he'd be a little short
It was something he couldn't deny us
Arms limp at his sides, he walked away

I like to imagine that he argued
That he cried in attempts to stay whole
That he held us in his arms
Tears streaking down his face
The look of a broken man
His face a setting sun melting into the ocean

I like to imagine that he called constantly
Trying to make amends to bridge the distance
That we were at the forefront of his mind
That he showed up uninvited
Diapers under one arm
A teddy bear under the other

I have a half-sister I've never met

That he walked away from first
Maybe she was the hardest
When my mom pointed at the door
It was like Pavlov ringing a bell
Without thought he found himself alone

I was left with a gaping hole in my chest
A severed, invisible umbilical
Trailing out behind me
The weight of a logging chain
Leaving a trail of black bile
For most of my life

My father reentered my life a few years later
Reaffirming a bond I always knew I needed
A puzzle piece fitting my chest hole perfectly
I no longer dragged that logging chain
Though I no longer envied other children
I had gained a friend in him more than a father

I think he felt that he gave up that right
That it would be a waste of time anyway
When so much joy was had just being friends
And when life was a storm he was a safe port
Two years ago a storm washed away that port
I'm often come undone at the thought of this

Looking at my two-year-old son
I imagine the hole in his chest
That I can only fill with stories
Of his quirky, loving grandfather
That he'll have no memory of
And have to trust my recollection of him

At the same time I long for that lost period
The early years I didn't have my father
I look at my son
And I couldn't imagine walking away
I would level a city, sell my soul to the devil
To be by his side

As a child, brought up catholic
I believed in a heaven and hell
I've since stepped away from faith
And I put my belief in Socratic method
Which relies on student-teacher dialogue
I've lost my teacher but gained a student

Thinking of the loss of my father
My fading youth
My son's long journey ahead
I hope I'm wrong about heaven
I hope I'm wrong
When I have no choice but to…walk away

just survive somehow
Samantha Lucero

when they were unborn the attachment formed in water
with a beaded cupid's bow of drowsy baths.

where with that ruptured moon through acid-etched
windows, that hazy heaven-white circle in
a peerless, quiet moan gazed in, and you wept the way
you will when this absurd world darks,
and deaths curtain pulls you back.

I ferried you here,
and it's too late to swim back.
We've gotta survive together,
'til I leave you
To survive somehow.

but soon, the unborn squeeze out
and are born, they scream.

sometimes you scream back,
sometimes they cry and so do you.

you formed an attachment to someone
you never knew, who now you know,
and they know you.

Widow's Rock
Allie Nelson

The waters are like a widow's hair, black and lustrous
with lost foam of tears salted to rime, the ocean weeps
for her husband sky, now blackened with the rot of
night, for it is only when his sun is a coin in the sky
that mourning waters light with warmth, each day
the seas cry for sky's death, and hang the moon up
as a gravestone resplendent for his yellow eye.

the Yellow month
Lois Linkens

March is an oddly yellow sort of month,
A blushing Spot in Feb'ry's ice blue cheek.
January had its day, but gone's the plinth
From whence it stood. The year's regrets still shriek
In its sordid wake. But we are not there,
Not now. We have entered bright March, dear one –
The Marigold of months has sure begun.
Fling back the shutters and let down your Hair.
But – oh! What sights have gathered at the door?
What frozen horrors lie across the floor?
This is the Yellow month! I do despair,
The month of Daffodils, of gentle air.
Warming Breezes, the first young buds of Spring!
The damned white Snow has covered everything.

Song of Spring
Iulia Halatz

Spring is a princess
without voice
only fingers
to mix colors
in the rainbows.

She's got a vessel
for the softest fragrance
pressed in archives
in the Library of Scent...
There are plums
the cherries
and the blooms of vines
escalating
on the earth's shelves...

Anyone who writes down
to Spring
is simply wasting
a leaf of scent.

No one is ever so poor
as not to write up
music
to all the shades of Spring
and to the dancing stars
to give a gift
of chaos...

Ribeira dos Namorados – The Valentine Stream

Jonathan O'Farrell

Urging un-quieted falling, fluidity.
Senseless, surfing god torrent.
White noise cleansing oblivion.
Fluvial cold catharsis sender.
Rampant throwing moss-pit
Drenching doom spume.
Rampaging slit.
Delinquente deluge, slab slayer.
Forment shuddering orgasmic overthrow.
Aqueous aquarian revolt.
Spurting denyer of place.
Roaring rent in stability.
Quenching, opportune, outlet.
Cleansing cleft rock crusher.
Rudderless rushing lubricant.
Future, glistening, delight.
Riverine stage for summers lovers, owls and javeli.
Mount my vulnerable banks, engulf.

Greenen parlor
Iulia Halatz

What do you see when you look at night?
The kraken sleeping
in the murk
His thoughts
would change the color
of whom
he once abhorred.

The moon is faint
and builds
the hauberk
of bark
around the dark
with armatures
that are about
to conquer down
the light.

What do you see when you look at love?

Kraken kisses and embraces
of a woman of innocence
unwise, unadorned
untamed.
Slumbering in green tentacles
vividly electric
to pursue in night
unnumbered words
astray from his

wondrous grey
to host in the parlor
the Someone
they desired.

Her untamed soul
drags her love
like Simoom
grabs the grains of sand
in hurdles and pains.

We cannot step
outside love's iron songs.
Its music
brings falter
in the bones.
It is the alphabet
that guides the waters
to stay together
and roar
North of the wind
glisten
South of the sun…

Fall Flings

Marcia Weber

autumn
fickle lover
you tease an aging summer
fill her weary lungs
with the heated breath
of your lost abandon
toss your fiery colors
crinkled casts
of your passionate embrace
at the feet of her sun-soaked journey –
gold threaded vermillion carpets
cushion the heartache
of her grand exit.
your fingerling breezes
caress her flushed brow
dapple sour apple kisses
upon bronzed shoulders
stencil erotic promises
beneath the sinews
of her marching thighs.

autumn
tantric temptress
you entice a nubile winter
fill his cavernous pockets
with polished talismans
of your smoke- breathed vitality
denude yourself of finery
an offbeat up-tempo

strip tease
shivering limbs outstretched
quivering in anticipation
of a lovers' blanketing.
your razor nailed gusts
race in vixen bursts
grazing his arched spine
entice his withered furor
with amber beams
of half hooded coquetry
lingering languid
upon the clouded steel
of his stealthy advance.

Melt

Iulia Halatz

I have shared
land and sky
with you.
I have tasted
blood and honey.
My witch-oil turned
to dragon-fire
at your touch…

Soft fingers laid asleep
until your turmoil
woke them
for so long….

It feels like getting drunk
on old reddish wine
long softened
during times of
War
Equanimity
and
Comets.
What shall I pour in your glass?
Molten flowers
Golden ink
Lucid light
Unicorn mirth…

I dig your veins

for gold.
I find pure
bitter-sweet
amber nuggets.

I fear any story
whose ink
my words
can't drink…
Yet I drip in yours
ever since.

When your arms call
and your lips
read all my feral kisses
How can there be no heaven?

For Your Kiss
Max Meunier

i lay the braided stars
before your precious countenance
that you may walk
the path of light
where gods
no longer dwell
for we are but a figment
of ephemeral affectation
reflecting in the tear
that wells
in worlds
wont to forget
the season of surrender
shall not plunder my resolve
to beckon at your call
under the restless moon's fluoresce
awakened…
stripped and strung
in astral flecks
that flickered with foreboding
the myths depicted
in the dithering
of days foregone
still haunting,
as your fragrance wafts
into the garden
florid waifs found desiccant
wistful sentiments
entwine me

in an urgent yearning
for your kiss

All the days of my life

Jonathan O'Farrell

Not just one day,
all of the days I count.
And all of the ways I could count and remember,
I will and feel, in the depths, of me.
All the loves, in so many ways,
all precious and held.

in my heartwood I.
On my many branches, you and you.
And you, even you, Saint, you are in there
Not that I am a blind believer,
in all that dressing up,
love for one day held special.

Tending, feeding, watching over, preparing the new.
Oh but a few selected low hanging fruits
I am ever, each day, grateful.
For they add flavour to our already juicy lives
and the story, of all loves we tasted,
yet not consumed whole, any one.

Venusberg
Iulia Halatz

She walks slowly
like music
She feels gently
like water caressing
the stone it pierces
in the long haul of time…
The cleavage of a rose
tells all about her beauty.
Fine alabaster lies
In the heart of her skin.
Sweet fruits alive
in the deep velvet
of a green swirl
are dappled with her insurmountable scent.
She catches the tendrils of care
sent by your star
She buries them
in trenches
in her armature of love.
Your breath is
mortgaged to her smile…
Burnished sunsets
chant
the moment
She steps
in the shade of the evening:
"Can you dance on water with I?"

Out of My Hands
Matthew D. Eayre

The voices in my head
told me, today
they want to see other people
and I don't know
if I should be jealous
or happy
because I have been wanting
to hear new voices
for quite a while.

For a thousand-thousand years
my hands have held tightly
holding weapons of self-destruction
or bouquets of hope
squeezing the cold and unresponsive hands of life lost
too soon
clawing at dark and imaginary walls
prisoners of silent screams echoing through time.

My hands have caused pain,
and they've soothed wounds.
My hands have been instruments of wonder, building
legends from mist and recording prophecies in stone.

My hands have been unwelcome guests in my own
pockets, useless and despised.

Given a true purpose my hands become valuable,
irreplaceable tools.

My hands had never touched a home
until the day my secrets poured through the gate they
formed over my face, and into her endless eyes, trapped
by her attention my mind was a formless void
and she spoke, and all was light.

Raw ingredients in the hands of a culinary master know
the pleasure I felt that day, when she took my hands and
my pain and transformed me into a work of beauty, a
composition of cultured cohesion.

She had been waiting for my hands, my lifetime of a
thousand centuries clinging desperately to secrets, lonely
and aching.

She took me, her long-awaited love, and kissed my
wounds out of my hands, away from my brutish touch
and into the gentle garden of her care.

She lifted the veil of mortality from my eyes and
revealed to me my personal divinity, and in my
newfound godhood
she found her intentions and unspoken desires made alive
by my hands.

And I try harder at this than anything else, because every
heartbeat leaves an uncertain pause,
will this be the last?

How it feels to love another
more than you can explain to yourself
is a tiny taste of hope between breaths

lingering in the space where
nothing is permanent.

With ferocity and gentle administration
my hands have given what has never
been mine to keep, emptying thoughts and words,
passing around plates of poetry, plenty for everyone,
take what you will.

I've lived this dream long enough
to have absolute knowledge
that the eyes in my heart will close
the love I live will end

and she breathes and I
take it personally
when she mumbles in her sleep
I am convinced it must be a dream of me, of my touch.

And I know the song I want to sing, on the day she
leaves, I know the words I will say when she dies,
because I know that our love has terms and conditions,
there's an unknown expiration date.

One day, one of us will leave the other,
too soon, too soon, it will always be too soon, if it was a
million years away it would be too soon.

Until that day we enjoy what cannot last

We have fun. We laugh. We try. We give.
Honest and purposeful effort, all day every day. We put
aside our individual

"Right now"
And we focus on collective
"long-term"
We wake each day and steer the ship toward bedtime,
and we work on getting there together.

We have our problems, my hands are not the only ones
full of the past.
We've both carried too much.

We don't promise forever, we don't know how long this
universe will last, if it's real at all, if anything is real.

But, I tell her, I will find you,
no matter where you go.
She answers, I will wait,
no matter how long.

I know this love story seems familiar, you've heard the
tale a billion times and a part of your heart wants to
believe and a part of your mind knows it cannot be true
It's true.

And when I say she's different from anything you know,
I'm trying to make you understand that I've seen life,
I've searched the universe
She's nothing you've seen, she's nothing you will ever
see, a unique and private bit of magic, made only for me.
In her love I become everything.
I am only for her, nothing without her, incapable of
losing with her by my side.

When I say we have something special

I mean we have something that has never existed, in this life or any other, in any time or place, what we have has no common ground with any fairytale or legend, what we have is insanely solitary.

This is not rhetoric.
This is real, as real as my hands, as real as her hair wrapped in my hand, as real as her voice whispering fiercely in my ear, as real as I have never been away from her.

What I'm saying is that my past, my life, my damage, my hands and the hurt they hold are sacred in her love.

I'm telling you that I can die
right now, happy
blessed beyond belief

because she
because we

I'm saying
This life is perfect.

Say Yes.
S.K. Nicholas

We sleep outside to be closer to the stars and because when we make love and taste God you want him to see you as a soul and not just a body. Pyjamas not skirts. Flirtation not chitchat. Tigers, dragons. Sushi bars and wet lips. Dimples and your smile and the absence of you when you're not around and you're never around but I have my words and my words will become you and that's just how it is. The evenings are beer and wine and the warmth of your breath against my neck in the back of a taxi and then your arm around my waist in some bar with paintings on the wall I could paint with my dick. Falling off your chair, you snort with laughter and bite my ear while begging me to stop and carry on in the same breath. What's the worst thing about getting old? My hair going curly. The second worst thing? The knowledge that my mind and body are two different things and that the older I get the more conflict there will be between the two. Arguments. Frustration. To sleep. Would you sleep with me right now? Would you let me take off your socks and massage your feet while we sit in silence too drunk to do anything other than picture ourselves as different people? I do hope so. The beginning, the end. A writer, and a fool. A hand around your throat. A doorway that could be a vortex that could be a portal that could be an opening to something those we have known our entire lives have never come close to. Do you remember when we were strangers? Can you recall the time you caught me staring at your mouth in the canteen at work not long after you started? You asked me if I was okay, but I was lost in the future that danced upon your lips and although I didn't want to be crude, I knew already what was to follow and it caused me to become lightheaded. Two hearts. One mind. That night we were first under the stars and I wrote **GN-z11** on your arm with a pen and urged you to get it tattooed- you never knew what it meant and I never told you. Well this is the place we shall go after we die and there we shall be forever free. Type it into Wikipedia, and tell me you'll say yes.

upon realisation that perhaps i am completely sure
Lois Linkens

you weave your woollen whims
to surround me
in the gabardine of our gandering
you trample the simplicity
of tea-cup games and teddy bears –
playground grazes know none than this
damp shirt and glasses;
i'd switch my eyes for yours
so you could see
beneath the ocean
still, ride the blackwaters
with socked feet sodden;
put your records on
and leave paw prints around my petticoats
take me to the dock,
where the walrus wail
and seagulls cry.
let us know the purity of instinct
the purity of art
that transcends education,
memory or muse
you are scars and sculptures,
skin and silver
stonehenge me

Don't Over Text Me
Georgia Park

"I'm commitment phobic and I actually like you. I want to text you all the time and eat you out for hours and cook you dinner."

"Please do not over text me, I'm too busy."

"I'm gonna do it right now."

"That's silly. I'm standing right here, and I refuse to respond."

My phone vibrates, and I don't touch it. He smiles at me. It's very awkward. I have a giggle inside me that I'm hiding, for good reasons.

I look at him sternly, exhausted.

The Woman:
Nathan McCool

That woman is a lotus flower
balanced on the point of a diamond.
I dream of her roaming the shallows at
Ocean Springs
-her feet dancing on the water
like shimmering splinters of light.
She comes to find me
as a lotophage scarecrow etherized
in the full dark of all moonless nights.
She adorns me with shells for teeth
like pretty, sea scented candy; and
leaves her hair hanging softly from
my straw fingers.
That woman is a mythic creature
roaming wild in the marrow of my bones.
At all times I can hear her lullabies echoing
through these calcium caverns.
And I have found if I speak her name
I always desire to breathe it deep
back into my body
so it can resonate between my
languishing muscles and burning blood.
Heal me this last and final time.
My woman moves in my mind like a nebula
shifting between dimensions
with all the brilliance and beauty
of exploding stars and cosmic energy.
And you know I'd give myself
to the void of space if I might one day

find myself there,
immersed in the particles of her being.
I'd exist in the cold and the silence,
broken bodied and weightless,
if I could ever do such a thing to be truly worth
even her gaze.

A Big Nothing.

S.K. Nicholas

They say I'm not romantic, that I'm distant and distracted, but my love shows itself in many different forms. They tell me that I'm cold, that I don't know how to connect. My defense is that it's them- it's them that can't connect to me because they're not open to the ebb and flow of my myriad ways. Actually, no, it's me. I confess. I'm far too strange for those who happen to cross my sullen and maudlin path. Smoking my cigarette, I contemplate my actions but grow bored within the minute. Maybe sooner. My attention span isn't great at the best of times. There should be writing, should be declarations of love, and yet I keep thinking of all those roads from my childhood that don't exist anymore and the names of random galaxies I looked up on Wikipedia the other night after polishing off the rest of that red wine I'd been refusing to drink because white is just so much sweeter. Near where my grandparents lived in Lewsey Farm, there was an area of marshland that used to terrify me back when I would stay with them during the holidays as a kid. Not sure why it got under my skin, because it was all fenced off and secure and there was no chance of ever stumbling in. Yet for many years, I just couldn't help but worry that one day I was going to find myself in a terrible predicament. As the wine does its thing and the wheels in my brain begin to spin, I feel a thought coming on. Y'know, even though we barely speak, maybe we could pay the place a visit? One evening when you're not too busy wanting to break my bones, and it's not too cold, we could take a drive up and slip through a hole in the fence before exploring each other's bodies? I'm having trouble remembering the exact shape of your breasts, and every time I try picturing them I get these nosebleeds that just won't quit. Every time I close my eyes and taste your lips, there's a flavour that just won't shift. It's one of the skittles, maybe the blue one? Yeah, that's it. You're a blue skittle I want to suck and chew beneath a blood-red moon as the ground beneath us swallows us whole until there's nothing left but our giddy laughter that rattles through the streets like the screams of some long-forgotten knife fight back in the summer of '92.

Two by Two
Daffni Gingerich

I remember the day I closed my eyes and there he was, coaxing me out of my shell. He had already created a place for me. I guess it all could've been a trap but either way it pulled me in in a way I would be set free from my past and locked into infinity. And every day is a reminder that I'm ok. I scream and claw and remove the skin from beneath my nails. But life can't stop there. It won't, and when the show goes on, I'm more learned and possess a trust in myself that helps me endure. When I inhale, evil spirits come along with the good ones and I sift through them like a collection of pearls before I cast them back into my writing. Except when I'm drunk, that's when I grab the first and act on it passionately with little thought. Every act is a piece closer to understanding and every nights sleep a chance to come back from the dead. Where we go there's footprints and where we bloom, there's the scent of leftover sex and cigarettes. He's the connection, the bridge from one stairwell to another, and together, we're an ocean I long to swim in.

The Waiting Room
Georgia Park

How awkward is it to wait with my boyfriend
in a doctor's office when the chances of me being
pregnant
are 50/50? Not very. We set a timer that reaches
almost 40 minutes. I sit on his lap and he sings.
I wear a gown that ties in the back
three times over but still shows my ass
and I pose for pictures in it,
I think damn, I don't look half bad.

Repeat Offenders
Mick Hugh

There weren't any horizons past those hillsides when we met — close-quarters of narrow suburban roads, barking dogs and neighbors and the claustrophobic push of childhood homes. Get back indoors: our engines had failed us. College dropouts returning, strangers, watching old friends warily lost in TV dinners and home décor trends. Tell your mother to turn the TV down. We were both working in the mall, nerves grounded to full-time jobs, saving money for unmentioned dreams in the shoeboxes beneath our beds. You: beautiful and raw-lipped, disastrous past relationships; a wrecked car and a brain still reeling from three candy-coated months in Montreal. You hadn't lasted very long. Welcome back to the working world. Never had a twenty-something moved so quickly in a Chipotle kitchen. Drink with your sister, drink with your boyfriend, back home quietly hating the ceiling of your bunkbed: return to your work-week, overtime, preoccupied operating your tattered dreams. Myself: drunk on my mother's couch, all night, just to sleep all day and miss the regrets of warm sunlight. Suppress the screams from foreign lands. A collection of pens that wouldn't write, nightmares cutting tongues on eyelids, masturbating feverishly. Febrile seizures self-concocted. Please take a walk with me: An act of desperation. Cigarette conversations by the dumpsters on our breaks. You had a catch in your rhythm and you reeled me right in. Flirtatious, confident, naïve: we had everything for the two of us in a dream clamped tight in our hands. Love in a glass bottle we left on the roof, trunk packed with swimming clothes and summer shorts, miniskirts and additional cans of beer. Molly in the glove-compartment, books between the seats, playlist of 2016's best indie. Sun-baked August highways stretching, endless, towards new lands long-ago conquered by poets with faces in the stars. Duct-taped hearts, our hands tightly clamped and the quiet promises that inevitable errs wouldn't bring us to part, for we started this trip properly: that old glass jar left far behind in the pot-holed driveways of Home.

In Blues and Golds

Nicole Lyons

God, I am selfish.
I am a selfish lover,
and a selfish friend,
and I am a selfish saint.
But am I selfish on Sunday
when I break my bread
and remember that girl
and her tingles,
and every prayer I whispered,
when I was running
from scared into terrified?
I was unselfish when
I was terrified in that tunnel,
and I was high on those vibes
when we met.
The electric terror and tiptoes,
the sweet sound of bored teenagers
breaking trust and all the rules.
We smoked her stepfather's cigarettes
and drank my mother's wine,
and we spray-painted our names
inside each other's secrets
in golds and blues across dirty metal,
and then she laid me down.
I was unselfish and terrified
that time I said yes
when I meant to say no,
but her fingers were quick
when my resistance was weak,

and I was two seconds to thirteen
and a lifetime from knowing better.
And now I can't help but feel sorry
when I remember her then,
under those flickering lights
a block away from home,
and the way we kissed.
That kiss that stormed the skies.
That kiss that shook the plains.
That kiss that had her speaking
of tingles and first love,
and body rocks.
That kiss and those tingles,
on that body from a lifetime ago,
are now ravaged to bits
in a home somewhere,
eaten by the degenerate mouths
of degenerative diseases,
and here I am,
still selfish and terrified,
at breakfast on Sunday,
saying a prayer and wondering
if the tingles her body is wracked
and wrecked with now
can come close to the ones I gave her
in blues and golds, way back then.

Affliction
Kindra M. Austin

What do you mean to me? No
goddamned clue. But I know I'm
in deep blue like with you, boy,
when you stand on the corner
of nineteen hundred
and eighty-seven,
wearing black kohl eyes, and that
Robert Smith hair.
Toss me a menthol ciggie, then
take me by the hand;
pull me straight out of myself,
and into the back alley where
your beast heart beats.

Let me smear your painted lips
with my gin soaked tongue—
you're so fucking pretty.

Make me the object
of your affliction.

Semaphore
Jimmi Campkin

We build sandcastles just to destroy the pure, wet sand, dreaming of pineapples, messages in bottles and California. Suntanned toes and blue lipstick, red dyed hair that runs in the rain and streaks your shoulder blades with plastic blood. Lights twinkle over the harbour like your teeth in the sunlight. You attract men, flies and trouble, and all three irritate you and spoil your fun. You ask me, why can't we burn down the local chapel on a Sunday morning? And it isn't rhetorical. Hell hath no fury like an ex-Catholic.

Later that day, we conquer the sea. You remove your red panties and pierce them with a shank of driftwood, plunging it into the oncoming tide in the name of Us… and what a concept that seems to me sometimes. There is no Us, just You, hurtling around the Earth like a cannonball in the Hadron Collider, which you call the HardOn Collider whilst squeezing the blood out of my stiff cock, leaving it sore and limp like a dead chicken.

Today the sea is a flat plane of blue glass, and in the quiet the echoes are louder. Clouds rumble overhead, keeping watch but never staying long enough to enforce justice. I'm lying on my back as you fondle my balls with one hand and grip my neck with the other, asking me over and over again why I keep breathing. It's boring, apparently. Breathing is boring. I should just stop doing it. My friends say you aren't healthy for me. But one by one they are going out, like Christmas tree lights, and soon it will just be Us again… or maybe just You, rubbing powdered glass into the slice you made in my arm with a fish-gutting knife, because…. well, just *because*.

Mother's Blood

Mitch Green

Forever sorry, cut at the
bleach ghost in strokes.
Prove her out to be the
head over heels, smoke
em if you got em type.
Worming mists of steel,
sacrificial, superficial.
They warned you about
this one. They warned you,
stubborn listener.
They'll fish you
out in pieces.
Tell me it to be fiction,
cause on the third floor
a girl fits a cage, made
of roses, thorns, and her
mother's blood.

Pink Flamingos
Daffni Gingerich

I huff and puff and walk out. Stamping to my car I sit behind the wheel and curse him. I go to find gas station pizza, the two pack of Hostess' vanilla cupcakes, annnnd possibly a pint of ice cream that claims to be over loaded with fixins just to try and calm myself. I hate it when I walk in on him with other women. I mean I do disappear, no phone calls, and sparse emails with a few shallow lines of poetry to let him know I'm still breathing, but fuck put a sign on the door. And don't think of me when you're with her cuz that's just weird. Even though many times I've done it, even closed my eyes to seal the deal, but that doesn't matter. I tried to picture him beneath me, so vulnerable so fragile. And completely mine because I've straddled him and lassoed his thoughts so he'd never have to say he loved me out loud. But when I heard it echo through my brain I finished him off and left without saying goodbye. It was entirely too real. And we'd only seen each other a good 5 times outside of professional walls. Or maybe that was the first time, who's keepin track these days. I could only think of how large I'd felt and how such a manly man could shrink so small beneath me. Not his cock of course, that grew. What kind of woman would I feel like if it didn't. Then there's erectile dysfunctions and that makes me feel a kinda shitty too. So anyways he was rock hard and I was wet because it was my first time straddling him. I leaned in and placed my forehead on his after telling him I could read his mind. But he already knew and had I love you at the forefront, just behind his skull where all the executive

201

stuff is supposed to happen. So when I connected my head to his I felt entirely too much power. A man's life isn't mine to hold.

Because I am worth so much more

Sarah Doughty

"Because I am worth so much more.
I deserve better than loving
someone like you."

Maybe, loving you was wrong. Maybe, I knew that being
yours would end in my own heartbreak. But, darling, did
you ever consider that I made that choice on my own?
That you had no business putting words in my mouth —
words I never spoke. That you had no right to force my
actions. Or act upon your belief that it was in my best
interest. Maybe, this has been my problem all along.
Choosing to love someone that could never accept me for
who or what I am. Loving someone that I knew, deep
down, would never change. Maybe, I should have loved
myself more, respected myself more. Because I am worth
so much more. I deserve better than loving someone like
you.

Fawn

Jimmi Campkin

We'd convinced the girl behind the screen to let us climb the church tower. We were both stoned beyond human comprehension – only nature could understand us now – but with her bored expression and indigo hair, we could see a kindred spirit. Arms over shoulders we talked about the coming of the Lord, and how we needed to get really high, because we wanted to run our fingers through the clouds, and you kept spitting on the glass every time you tried to pronounce a hard 'th'. Never mind. Our tickets were punched, and I swear I caught a smile as a lock of dark purple hair curled over an ear pockmarked with empty piercings.

Up the narrow stone steps we wound, tripping over each others ankles, inhaling all the smells of history – damp, dust and decay. Emerging on a ledge, supported by one thousand year old masonry, we stared up at the same sun from all those ages ago, and ran our fingers through the grooves left by people long since lost. No tombs, no bones, no names, just the gashes in the rock. I carved our initials into the soft stone to continue the journey.

Your lapdance around the spire was bizarre. Uncoordinated. You stripped like a propeller rather than a dancer, flinging clothes and limbs everywhere. Quoting The Dane, you screamed into the air; I have of late, wherefore I know not, lost all my mirth...

I sat down, watching you self-destruct, what a piece of work…

Madness
Sarah Doughty

I'm more than ordinary madness. I'm not a temporary fix, but I am your devil in disguise. That desire setting you to burn like liquid fire flowing through your veins. Let me make you my paper and write all night with ink on my tongue, inciting those flames to grow. Then you'll never want anything else.

Street Rats
Daffni Gingerich

From the depths of my churning stomach, he pulls out my childhood and makes me puke so violently it comes out of my eyes. After wiping my face, he kisses my acidic lips. That's when the world stops and the words start to fall out of me. The mustard plants in the vineyard across the street bloom yearly. They're beautiful so I sit on the fence and get lost in them. When with me, he'd stare for a good 20 mins before sneaking his dirty paws up my shirt. The wind would cause me to run through the flowers in whatever direction it blew. The sky is blue and I can taste grapefruits in the air. He grabs my arm and pulls me back towards him to say I could never get away. With his arms locked tight around me and my soul devoured by his eyes, I feel a shiver go up my dress. Reminds me of Clara Harris, the woman who they claimed had "sudden passion" and hit her husband repeatedly with a car. Then proceeded to run over his lifeless body. His kisses bring me to places I never planned on going. A monkey and tiger tug at my dress and the sultan rubs a gold lamp. I want the lamp but when I return to his kiss there's not much else I could ask for. Besides well written work and well, that's something I prefer to earn over rubbing a lamp to get for free.

Painted Fingernails

Jimmi Campkin

Everytime I go to bed, I can see the stain of green hair dye on the low ceiling, where you cracked your head whilst vigorously riding me – yelping, eyes clamped shut and a gaping smile on your face, sucking up all the oxygen in the room and leaving me gasping for spare atoms. Of course, you were thinking of someone else the entire fuck, I knew that even at the time, but beggars can't be choosers. I didn't choose to worship you. I'm an atheist. I didn't plan on worshiping anything.

But as something tangible, you seemed a better bet than a concept designed to keep a feeble species in line. You kept me in line. And as feeble as I may also be, at least I could run my fingers down your stretchmarks; I could drag my nail over the little serrated dimples on your thighs; I could play with that mole on your hip and wonder at how it is surrounded by several smaller ones, a little solar system almost permanently hidden by the elastic of your underwear.

My deity was flesh; three day old mascara, a taste of cigarettes and last night's bourbon and coke, with dark circles under your eyes from dancing your legs down to the knees, and the smell of the smoke machine in your greasy hair. After the end, I spent many evenings in that club, dancing with other girls whilst watching you over their shoulders – dancing alone, happily not giving a fuck.

The Archer and The Scorpion
Kindra M. Austin

I found a photo of us, eight years old, stored in my 'sent messages.' We're sat at Tokyo smoking a cigarillo, looking utterly chuffed with ourselves. I thought I had destroyed all evidence of the Archer and the Scorpion union. God*damn*, darling, we made a fucking stunning couple when we stepped out dressed in gangster black, and with a dirty day drink buzz-on. But we were stunninger in the dark, when you worshipped at Church of Me; your platform bed served well as altar. 2 a.m. moon soaked Liturgy, my sweet heathen, you were no atheist sheathed in my silk.

Addict
Allie Nelson

It's evening, and we're both drunk as stoned birds, and
you look like a young Hannibal Lecter and stink of
corpses and rotting roses. I'm in bandages and heels, I
cut myself on your broken bottles again, maybe because I
hate myself or maybe because I hate you and I want you
to see your precious little canary bleed red, dead,
showing the coal mine of your palace is stranger danger.
There's needle pricks along your forearm and you're
ranting and raving about how I left you for your brother,
the Prodigal Sun, and you're the fuckup your dad kicked
to the curb into a joint you call Hell with your bachelor
buddies where all you do is fuck and kill and get high
any means possible. I say your twin is worth a thousand
yous and I'd rather you were dead by my hands than
calling me jezebel and heirodule and all your pretty
words for whore. Maybe you get off on me sleeping with
all your friends and enemies – no, I know you do,
because you own me and I own you and I only do as we
please and you're a manwhore that likes used goods –
but for now you're pretending it's only us at night, not
succubi or angels of prostitution or all the fancy terms
rabbis came up for cheap ladies of the night that dress up
in oxblood lipstick and leather and decorate your palace.
I tried to join in on one of your orgies once and you
laughed to high heaven at how innocent I was, too pure,
and your wives stroked my hair and tweaked my nose
and then you got back to your fucking. So much for
sharing. I don't know a damn thing about drugs and all
the shit you drink and snort and smoke and siphon

210

through your veins but silver daggers are pumping this clear heady substance into your banded arms and I'm cornered, horny, and pissed. I imagine you are the same, because what fucking loser castigates his wife for straying and throws temper tantrums then comes crawling back drunk for forgiveness and pleads for a second chance, a millionth chance, just take my poetry and books and roses and shittily made tacos and let's pretend I'm the dragon, you're the princess, and your fucking knight brother was burned to a crisp. You grab me from behind and I hike up the bandages and you talk about kids and how pretty I would be pregnant and I tell you to fuck off as I cum and you're still snorting coke off my spine and we rut until I bleed and you're raw. You mock me for missing a spot waxing but I know you'd fuck me if I had a sixties porno bush. You've made it a point to fuck me however I look, lathering me up to a soap with compliments and moaning and weakness as your seed spills out and I could sink my teeth into your manhood and drink down all the black sin inside you. You're crying again, sobbing into my hair, saying how could I have left you for the better half, the sober one, the brother you hate and love in equal measure. I tell you to shut the hell up and let me sleep and that I only keep you around because you're hot when you're not an abomination. I'm pretty sure you raised me to kill you, and you love watching me in other men's arms, but then you go and haunt my boyfriends and fuck me in their beds so who knows. All I know is that you think you have me figured out, but then I go and surprise you and you lose your shit and rant and rave like a rabid dog. Watchdog of the graveyard, you called yourself. The Scapegoat. Samuel the Judge. I hope the whole fucking

211

Internet reads this and the Satanists know what a pussy their god is. The Devil's a cuckold and cries at Victor Hugo and beats his women and is as disturbed as his favorite eponymous band. Addict Angel Extraordinaire. Waste of Space Junkie. This is just me spewing shit on the page to see what sticks but isn't that what I always do?

I learned to write from you, after all.

Wasps
Jimmi Campkin

Open up my skull and you will find her inside, in a tatty
striped dress and muddy Doc Martens. Every bedroom,
every hotel room, every airport lounge, train and coach I
sleep in she is there, smiling and licking razor
blades. When I shower I look into the steamed mirror
and see a pair of blue eyes staring back at me. Neither of
these eyes belong to my partner. *She* is still there, with a
red flowing tongue and a black choker.

This is no guardian angel. She is guilt and sex and
violence, with greasy hair and furry teeth - not brushed
since her last remembered birthday and
she *always* forgets her anniversaries. Years later, lying
in bed next to my partner, 'the woman I love', I wait until
I hear gentle snoring before I rest my head on the pillow
and close my eyes. I know that I talk in my sleep, and all
I think about is Her, with a mouth full of blood and
bacteria. In my lucid dreams I feel the hairs on my face
lift to receive that sour taste. I feel my pupils expand,
opening like bank vault doors to a secret code.

As teenagers together, she took me to her secret place - a
single tree in a circle of thick thorn bushes. Like a
ballerina she danced up to a noose tied to a low branch,
launched her head inside like a basketball three-pointer
and thrashed - piss streaming like river deltas down her
soiled, writhing legs as I watched, frozen in a moment of
incredulous horror. After a few moments she lowered
herself down and her barefoot heels touched terra firma.

213

She stood before me, at her full height, the rope now slack at her shoulders. There was no danger, it was all a game. Removing the noose, she walked towards me. *You never even tried to save me* she smiled, and kissed me hard. It tasted disgusting. And then she kneed me firmly in the groin.

I sank to my haunches; coughing and farting, with a stomach ache billowing through my insides. Looking down at the floor I saw brown leaves, dead twigs and ten toes with ten filthy toenails. I thought to myself; *I wonder if my tongue could clean these grey stumps?* A few minutes later, I knew the answer....

Daffodils
Olde Punk

The smell of rotting agendas always waft in your wake. I've grown accustomed to your sand storm daffodils. It's not what you once were, but what you could be that still intrigues me. Potential, potentially terminal, with velocity. Sniper taking aim, the looks you throw with abandon. I lie still sometimes and pretend I can hear the screaming in your eyes. I would have given it all for you, you know. I do not think it would have mattered to you. You are the song Reptile by The Church. I can see you sauntering and stalking in the sun by the beach every time I hear that song. Which is often, 'cause I like to pick at open wounds. The bloody mouth of puckering pink skin attempting to heal is such a turn on and a visceral reminder of your violence, my violet-skinned lecher. Your Krispy Kreme coochy-coos hardening my arteries. And then, slow syrupy suicidal sex. Something in me went dormant when you left. I vaguely remember why, but it's fuzzy like flash backs from a blackout or a bad trip. Which I only had once or twice, but that was more than enough to keep from doing it again. I would for you though, if you wanted to. Crashing around in the forest at dusk under deep November skies and yelling fuck-all to the universe. You were always the spark that started Devil's Night. A goddess of Bacchus' loins. There was nothing I would not have done for you. I died when you left. The husk remains, with the frozen portraits of your jack o'lantern smile burned into my retinas. My skin still shudders with the traces of your touch. My gypsy witch, evil love cursing the hearts around you like a speedball on fentanyl on meth that is the last run of the roller coaster and heart is pounding and I will be with you soon and my veins are flame and my heart is a jackhammer and I will be in you soon and I will kill you soon and soon I am coming for you my beautiful malady with the melody of death on my lips... and a fistful of sand storm daffodils.

216

Minotaur
Lois Linkens

should i burn for you?
sacrifice myself for you?
leave behind my friends for you,
become something i'm not for you?
eat away my heart for you,
wrap my soul in cloth for you,
be a real woman too,
a real woman, through and through.
should i be a bitch for you?
make up pretty lies for you?
convince my mum i'm fine for you,
just because you want me to,
stay behind the line for you?
at your feet i pay my due.
on grazed knees await my cue,
desires and whims i must subdue,
i owe my everything to you.
in death, in life, i'm chained to you,
polished, prepped and preened for you,
i am the other half of you.
we make a pretty pair, we two,
a minotaur we are, us two,
man and bull, stuck up with glue.
i am the bull that leads us through,
i am the head and frontal view,
all i want is to please you.
all i want is to please you.
all i want is to please you –
and you, in turn, will love me too?

for all of our forever, won't you?

In Waiting
Kindra M. Austin

I waited at the back of his throat—
waited to hear him confess my name so I could come out
from behind his teeth, and defend my claim
over him. Illusory love o' mine
kept me cleaving to the bitter of his tongue; for all of her
disdain he swallowed, I did
wash in, waiting.

We used to get shit-faced, and fuck each other mad,
down by the river in
dew slick grass,
monstrous 'neath the white-gold moon.

He'd give it to me good 'til I was
howling, and scratching
bloodstained claws at that discerning watch
slung up high in sleeping cerulean.

I waited at the back of his throat—
waited for him to confess my name.
He didn't.

Every time he chokes, he's reminded of me.

Runaway Train

Laurie Wise

Hell bent on wiping me out
You've seen me fall before
Reached out and offered a hand
Now you shove me out the door
Desperate attempt to even the score
Radio silence
You aren't right all the time
Living on urban vapors
Poisoning your mind
Evaporating
Hearts of the kind
A story of revenge
Veiled in resurrection
Force you to look in my direction
Fiery Armageddon
Made a sovereign decision
Retracted my open invitation
This isn't a journey
It's a runaway train
Tracks rusted and eroded
Mirroring damaged brain
No light at the end of the tunnel
The temple has been set on fire
Crucifix burned across my chest
Tortuous desire
There is no day of rest
This isn't a test
Rooted in utero
Nourished with disease

Fed on sacramental fear
Born to bleed
I cannot descend any further
Screams heard only by the captive
We speak in secret tongues
Ghosts of when we were young
Nature knows no mercy
To pray is to accept defeat
Buried under deceit
Assassin in the afterlife
Wrapped in caution tape
Tripping over dead bodies
Soak up the blood with a sponge
Served at ceremonial feast
Colluded with the beast
Patterned chaos
Open casket
Forfeit the win
Parasitic twin

Let Old Bones Lie
Nicole Lyons

I never could tell
if it was my body
or my mind
he ached to strip.
He had a weakness
for pretty disasters
and ugly tragedies.
The cut
of his tongue
sliced through both.
Colors exploded
into me, violent
shades of him,
striking my soul.

Hush
your quaking
heart,
we have many
things to see.

Calling
rings hollow now
on the heels
Of those
violent bells.

Let old bones
lie, I will
cut you
fresh roses.

Draw the cold
from my bones
and break me,
again. He was
the sweetest
regret I ever had
to swallow.

a conversation with a lover and a woman in love

Ra'ahe Khayat

i.
eleven days after she fell in love,
she told me-
"you've covered your body with bricks,
and i don't know if you're burying yourself
or the skeletons of all those sparrows
jay tucked in your pulse points
when he left."

"he left me my poems in their coffins"
i said.

and he did.

he left me words that left
like his voice did,
as if
i was too unsatisfying a lover-
as if i'd slept with far too many shades of the sky
dealing with far too many breakdowns,
to ever be of worth to them.

ii.
an hour into the night,
she told me
how she was in love
with a boy in pressed shirts and tangled tongues,
and movie names scripted on his forearms,

and fairytales in his heart-

who held her as if she simply
was myriad.

and she said,
she loved him like i have only ever
longed for jay.

and that night, i never told her,
how most loves-
end;
and most lovers
become those who long
were;

because

she'd yet to learn.

iii.
i used to wake up
with a jay-bird perched on my left breast
pecking at the freckles on my clavicle-

saying he could taste
quasars dying on my skin,

before diving into the valley over my sternum,
breathing
like he was a monk
starving for the air of a woman
bathed in the scent

of sex.

i was a virgin to his body.

and then,
he painted over me for three afternoons-
like the world was running out of tragedies,
and two anonymous lovers were
breaking out of stories,
and we-
were losing memories to fuck ourselves to

when we finally untangled
from this uncensored longing.

on the fourth day he told me-

"your skin is without being.

the bronze on your nerves
rots the death in my marrow;
while the black of your eyes
corrodes the blue in my lips
and this cold is far too fickle for me
to remain."

and so he was gone like most seasons are in august-
his body full of bones,
rattling like ceramic bangles do
against the wrist of a woman
trying to hold in her grief.

iv.
i'd never mentioned to her how a bird broke me
while she
fell for man.

Into My Arms
Nathan McCool

The place where I gathered all our hopeless dreams
only to bear witness to each of them devouring another.
My arms that always failed
to protect the things I cared about.
All of it was useless in the end wasn't it?

I would take back the mistakes if I could.
I'd run through the world to come and
kick down your door,
just a torrid, dreaming vagabond
smoking lithium from a lotus flower.
I'd say, "I'm here, my darlin. I'm here for good."

But things never turned out the way we thought they
should,
and our hearts are still just opposite horizons
torn in half by the same savage splinter of lightning.

I still dream of you swaying to my music
as you balance yourself on this piano.
I am still haunted by all the things in this world
that remind me of you.
I still sing songs
that offer you my melancholy love
and the hope that this world does not change you,
my dearest.
And if I could, Virgo,
I'd bring you into my arms
and tell you that I always did love you.

I'd tell you that, no matter the paths we take,
I always will.

A picture of our torn up praise
Aakriti Kuntal

Your absence is a theater. I grow disproportionate in it.
The winding and unwinding of curtains.
Warm air circulating through my face.
I imagine your body is no more a landscape.
That now it's a home. A home with
movements and sounds and occupants.
Your arms stretching your lover's slender body
into a lunar eclipse,
tirelessly eroding my feeble song. My tiny insignificant
memory.
There's been no word from you. Not even a sound.
It is as if your mouth transformed into a black hole
and took the rest of you too.
And I,
only I walk inside it.
Retracing my steps to see if I can
find any palpitating remains of us.
Anything, anything at all
that would explain
these patterned nights, these long long pauses in daylight.
How life has blatantly refused to comply anymore .
And how it has floated to some corner
of the nether sphere
where the sole thought of you is celebrated in adamant
silence.
Where even you would now be barred from entering.
Where only I sit
with our sick wobbly songs sprawled all over my lap.
My lucid legs dancing to the tune of your voice.

Widening into a continuous void.
All stars, all planets sucked in.
And I, I all alone,
All alone by myself baby
thinking about us.
Thinking of this throbbing universe of
endless possibilities where we could just not be.

Blu-tac
Lois Linkens

i will wipe your lipstick from the glass,
scrub the rings
off the coffee table,
and throw out the toothbrush and its plastic mug,
that sat
balanced on the sink
like a rock
on a cliffside
as if it paid rent.

you always knocked it off,
with your baggy sleeves –
you'd wet your hair
when you rinsed your mouth.
it was cold when you kissed me.

i will take your photo out of its frame,
and move your letters from the drawer.
i want to leave your diary by the bed –
if you visit, you could leave me a note,
if you wanted.
every day i have checked –
but the pages still are empty.
i will throw it out.

but
i will leave
the little knob of sticky tack
stuck above your desk

by the picture of bowie,
your fingerprint engraved
in the soft dip
pressed on its light blue skin.

i will leave it there,
because though others may wear lipstick
and drink coffee
and write poems,
your fingerprint
is the one thing i have
that could only be made
by you.

One More Time
Richard Crandall

My heart is torn in two
It'll eat you alive if you let it
let it take you
let it take you away

Within my dreams
it can drag you down if you let it
let it take you
let it take you away

All the lights have gone out
And a new day fades don't forget it
it will take you
let it take you away

I had this dream where I fall
and I can't get back up again
just acquaintances there
and nobody knows who you are

The dust on the floors have settled
to soot
it'll swallow you whole and
you'll never come back
you let it take you
take you away
you let it
don't you

This is the End

Aakriti Kuntal

We want to reach out.
But baby
here, now, this is the end.
We know, we know ' the end '. We've lived inside it.
Slept. Slept. Inhaled.
Creatures of absence.
Your eye is an alien being.
It alone sings. A rotating rim.
Continuously revolving in the hemisphere's strange
music.
I look down. My feet are shadows.
As are my thighs. My body. My bones.
All flesh is a memory.
I see its desperation in the starched sky.
I am the remainder. The remainder of distortion. Climate
of mishaps.
I say this is the end.
Your fingers tackle my defeated hair. You wish for
sound.
You almost demand it.
But I only meet you in clever silence. The loudest kind.
The ugliest kind.
I meet you in suffering.
You wish for me to speak.
Tell you that I love you.
But I only dissolve. I dissolve like all matter does.
In inconspicuous battles. I'm almost fluid. I almost do
not exist.
My face is streaming into yours.

My hands clasp yours and forge starfishes.
We are satin blue.
I hold you close to my mouth and kiss your bright skin.
Your mouth melts off
and your voice floats like snow flakes in my chest.
'This is the end.'
It says 'this is the end.'

Puppets and Preachers

Allie Nelson

Puppets and preachers line the hordes of back-alley
doctors,
It is midnight and the ground is cold as dead bones,
needles
Are on display as junkies shoot up in Harlem blue
hoodies,
You left me a long time ago, my love, a heart's harvest
Sown to rot, apple orchards bent to weary burdens,
And I cannot fix you, cannot claim you as dependent
On my back, I cannot carry you across the gulf between,
And we are islands and lighthouses, beaming sorrow
In a stream of white through the fog, no tomorrow.
I will tear this whole town down and dance on corpses
Like Shakti her Shiva, turned bloodlust to black Kali,
You are Shava the carrion charnel king, heartbroken
Though I have filled your wine glass to the brim,
When you squirm, my love overflows, you drown.

Lost Voice

Christine E. Ray

siren's golden voice
once dropped confident syllables
into air
as naturally as breathing
now stifled in constricted throat
that struggles to swallow
six-sided anxiety
hot, sour bile
college ruled notebooks
once full
of manic scribblings
compulsively captured in black ink
before inspiration could swirl down the floor drain
collect dust
sigh from disuse
pen now held in death grip
fingers have lost their grace
their nerve
fertile mind now an empty room
where silence rings
torturous tinnitus
blindfolded by fear
weight pressing down on shoulders
by the weight of giant
unseen inquisitor's voice barks
Have you reached the bottom of yourself
are you so shallow
so barren?!
Or is truth so deeply hidden

that you must dive inside
hand to elbow buried into slippery entails
to reach it?
surgical implements laid out
with precision on a stainless tray
slide into view
no hesitation picking up sharp scalpel
with shaking fingers
a writer's way is
always to bleed

Funeral Trumpets

Kindra Austin

With each jug of spirits
I ingest,
my organs' mourning
does crescendo; and premature
funeral trumpets
bleat in stereo, stricken on the sidelines of
my mind.

Every time I get sober,
someone else
dyes
black
my hair.

Skeleton Tree
Aakriti Kuntal

This evening
the hibiscus stands trimmed
Its head gone, chased
away
by winter's cold eyes

I swallow you like thick fog,
an anticipated dilation in all motion
It is
as if
all life has suddenly decided
that it must mourn and that
this mourning must never stop

That you must be worn like camouflage
And carried within the flicker of my violet iris
as it glides over uncertain nights
Hidden under warm rings of hurting fingers
and soft lullabies that only touch can penetrate

You must be laid flat
against the circling tide of age
and fervently loved against
all of life's failures
Left unbridled to hum
beneath every dreaming blade of grass
and whimper
against Nick Cave's vacating voices

241

That you must be
killed
over and over and over
Then recycled, redrawn, reborn
The memory of you circulating
in my overflowing skin, my autumn tissues,
my plastic timeline
Like a curriculum
Interspersed with chapters, ink, poems,
letters,
The library of our beloved corpses

Upon the Anniversary of Your Death

Jasper Kerkau

I carried your books—Mencken, Nietzsche, and other misanthropist tomes—boxed up and sold by the pound, exorcising all your existential angst. The body still warm, I drove your mother in silence to bookstore, trivial task, your prized possessions discarded in the abyss, torn covers and scribbled footnotes heralding a new aeon. Ten years removed, I am still touched by unforgivable grief, remembering your deep laughter and explosive spark— the glass-smashing, room-clearing nihilism that left fragments of strangeness everywhere.

I carried your grief, standing in your place, eulogizing your father and all the sadness in the world. I thought of your heartbreak, his rheumatoid-afflicted limbs, the never-ending horror of merciless suffering that drove you into nothingness as he wasted away. My shoes too tight, among strangers, swallowing my tongue, perspiring, hiding under table, echoing *I can do this…I can do this…I have to do this for him.* Tie crooked, I shake hands with your family—"thank you for standing in for him," they tell me with a wink and pat on the back. I bury my face in my hands afterward in the car. I will never again speak over the dead.

I carried your energy with me into adulthood. Swimming in blue waters, experiencing the miracle of childbirth, thinking of your eternal resignation—Methadone and Xanax—as I pass out cigars. I can't help but think that a child would have saved you, as I see the future in the

243

helpless innocence of my fruit. I "bought in," pushing carts down long aisles, groceries, comfort, pitter-patter of little feet, bank accounts, and Sundays strolling through antique stores. All the while, I feel the spectre of your life casting its pall over my experience. The sadness is at arm's length, though I know one day we will drink from the mead horn in the great hall.

I carried your failure with me through tragedy, running in circles, ankles and knees aching, never stopping…jogging past your childhood home. Finding God at the worst times, finding life in the place where you surrendered. *She walked out and you died.* I thought of this when mine left, rose from the dead, evolved, while you lingered in my shallow sleeps, haunting me as I struggled to overcome. Every day I pushed myself further away from that place you created. I was only an inch away, pushed into the shadows only to embrace the light. I did it because you could not—I did it for you.

I carried your passion, your love of knowledge, finished a degree, never walked but hid in bathroom at work, thought of you as I visualized them calling my name. "It was all for naught," I tell friends, secretly, of course, it was for you. Your brittle life redeemed by the marrow and bone pulverized and ingested in magic concoctions, secret rituals, great revelations thrown up in silly rooms with people I never knew as well as you. I bear the cross that people will never understand, never letting go—making the life that we dreamed of in the dreadful three a.m.'s when there were too many lines and too much talk that was all so fleeting.

244

I carried your beauty, your friendship, your combustible insanity with me. Sat on couches, bored, trying to find that madness, but I am cursed forever to a life of mundane drinks and civil discourse, dreaming of the past. I ask your mother if they ever got a tombstone. I think of your brilliance, unmarked, given over to eternity and worms—forgotten. My life is defined by you, looking forward, being better, not being swallowed by the same monsters that carried you away. You are with me in my dreams. After ten years, I think of you every day.

Intentional Amnesia
Matthew D Eayre

I keep having dreams with a recurring theme, different places and situations but one thing is the same
I'm sitting with my sister, the one that died 19 months ago, and I'm telling her how sad I've been about my sister dying.
She tells me things like,
she's still with you
and
you'll never really lose her
and all the while, we skip right past the part where I'm discussing the death of my sister, with my dead sister,
we never talk about the fact that my sister is sitting with me and holding my arm and comforting me while I'm crying about her dying

Once we were in a house that felt like home, even though I didn't recognize it, and she sat next to me and rested her head on my shoulder while all of my deceased friends and family members walked by and smiled at us
I'm not a religious person but I am fond of symbols and symmetrical concepts
One time we were at a jungle resort and my dead sister was talking to my dead grandmother while they sat on either side of me, each holding my hand

I've tried so hard to let go of all of my selfishness, but the weight of these metaphorical chains has been fused to my imaginary bones

I don't need a $400 an hour therapist to hold my hand and walk me across the street to the realization that survivor's guilt is truly a matter of selfishness
I wanted them to be alive, for me
Loving someone, or a lot of people, comes with a sense of permanence, but nothing could stray farther from reality
We have our moments, we have our days and sometimes we have our years, but the cold hard truth is that life is not permanent, not one of the people you love will be around forever, you and all the people you know will pass from this dream like a snowflake falling in Houston

I have a deeply embedded program in my mind that reminds me constantly that I'm sad about the days gone by, my favorite dead people ended on that day, and that day, and that day and the calendar is littered with morbid anniversaries and I count from one to the next like some demented accountant, a scribe recording the passage of time measured in unresolved guilt and I can't seem to sleep without sixteen dead people visiting me

I've been told that you only die once and that certainly feels accurate but I can tell you without any doubt that after you die the people that love you,
If they're like me,
Will feel like you died every damn day
They'll walk around their lives and they'll pretend to heal and they'll even find new ways to laugh and enjoy life but every time they dream of their sister or mother or nephew or brother telling them
Assuring them in a dream-like fashion that they still exist, that love hasn't ever died and never will

Every time your people wake up after you die, you will have died all over again.
Every day will be spent choosing to push aside the memories of your funeral or the unspoken words that will not reach your ears

Your people will choose to forget, while they're awake

They say that they're choosing to focus on the here-and-now, trying to live for what is coming, trying to let go and let God, trying to adapt to the new reality

But if they're like me

They'll be lying
They'll be dying your death in their head every time 'that' song comes on
They'll be wishing for a brain injury that causes permanent amnesia, just to get to a life that doesn't feel like death
They'll be trying to move forward with both hands and feet tied to the anchors of yesterday's ships

If they're like me

It's no comfort
Samantha Lucero

It's no comfort knowing that you're buried,
deep down, taking earth around you
like blankets that fall apart and crawl.

But seasons still disrobed like actors
backstage in a play, in front of
everyone. Even with you
gone, the world moved on.
And I watched. We all did.
Forced to watch, without you,
with seasons pouring the years
between us in vanishing old flannel,
smelling like Salem filter kings,
Soft.

Spring grew through us both
like a blade.
And you died in the summer.

A diamond in that box
they buried you in, deep down,
where you fall apart and crawl, too,
by now. Still waiting to be proposed,
like the plan to go back to Santa Fe.

Sometimes I wait for you to show,
maybe at the movie I go to alone,
sitting next to me when I peek over
in the flickering dark.

You could come around a corner
on a walk, and
not even say hello.

When I die, leave my eyes wide open
let them see that I'm dead.
Then burn me,
take my ashes to the Burren
where the wind will tear me apart
and take me farther away.
And my daughters can't go to my
grave and wonder
Is she alive down there?
Please be alive,
somewhere.

They can breathe me in
Or taste me instead.
when they lick their lips
after swimming in the sea.

And you'll still be in that box,
waiting to go back to Santa Fe.

Your Absence Is A Burglar
Kindra M. Austin

I'm running out of poetry; your Absence is a burglar of words and rhythm. You're the one who'd always told me to write my heart out. *Just write, baby girl.* Tell me, how am I supposed to cope with the loss of my goddamned verses? Who am I, if not a writer?

***

I wandered way down cobblestone,
deep in fog exhaled from lungs.
Mourning mind preoccupied,
my flitting feet followed instinct—
landed me at Dimwit dive-bar,
Old Town.
Somehow,
I ended up supping a ginny Gin Rickey.

Stood
in the nook at the
billiards table, a beatnik boy-toy of
Nimoy stature floated me a
hawk-eye look; affixed a fag to
his bottom lip, and
I just knew he was the type who
liked
Wuthering fucking Heights.

***

What comes next? I have an idea, but can't seem to execute it. I've been staring at this piece of shit for five wasted days. I'm too consumed with thoughts of you. And damn it, I'd like to be able to write about some other things now and again—in between fits of losing my mind over visions of you alone on the kitchen floor, and your blank eyes staring into nothingness. Shit, I'd like to put head to pillow at night without having to recall the scent of death that cleaved to your apartment despite the bottles of bleach that were used to clean up your leaked fluids.

Mother, what am I supposed to do? I'm so fucking tired of writing about you.

But who am I, if not a writer?

Murder in the thirst
Oldepunk

Murder in the thirst
There is always the murmuring first
Anticipation is just the worst
Do you not think?
No do not speak
Why we brave the waste
There is ever aught but dust
And folly, ever the tides rush
Close to our feet
I'm trapped in the past
And I know you are the last
Of the crimson knights of defeat
Feel my heart beat
In time with the rhythm of demise
I despise and deplore
Blood on the floor and all over
Your precious face
Oh angel of disgrace
Never are you more beautiful
Than with the fear of death
Perfuming your breath
And heavy with the knowledge
Of my damned divine curse
Shadow clouds over the moon
As dawn and dusk meet
Clasping hands over the finality
I embrace you lovingly
The taste of your blood on my tongue
I listen to the dearest murmur

That escapes your lips
And quench the murder
In the thirst

Gag Reflex

S. K. Nicholas

Triptych personality and a taste for the beaten and crushed. Favoured positions. Preferred imagery including a crushed butterfly placed so sweetly on her navel- the one that swims with my seed. Specks of blood on the bed sheets from our collision- the one I try denying but keeps happening anyway. In lipstick upon the wall, I scrawl my desires in lowercase. I spell out what I mean to say which always seems to escape me when she's gagging on my fumes. I'm a good guy at heart, but a single droplet puts me in a rage like you wouldn't believe. Shards of glass and portals. Lonely roads and stories gathering dust, but there will come a day when everything makes sense. There will be a moment when the end is not the end and an exit is not an exit but a door to a river where resides the girl who started it all. I go in and out- I pass through on the off chance she's around. Lights and nipples and stretch marks. Torn lingerie and tourniquets. Vampires, lovers, killers. A painter, a writer. There exists celluloid imagery of my actions. There are photos of body parts and vials full of hair which fuels the fantasy more and more. There was once a golden light but it was snatched away and now I take from others because my future was taken from me. Souls and slaves. The ties that bind. Scenes missing until she's wrapped in a blanket because this world doesn't care and although my hands are cruel I do it because I care and no one cares as much as me. She is mother and enemy. She offers salvation and torment but the more I do it the less I can tell which is which. Flowers pressed in a book. Numbed fingers from two bottles of wine as she shaves her pubic hair at my request. She is not her own woman, she is my girl. The girl by the river who visits me after I pass out in the early hours of the morning halfway up the stairs. She flickers in the eyes of those who get too close. She dances in the mirror and kisses my neck when the right scent ignites what's left of me. That cherub heart, it's been gone for years and no matter what I do, and no matter how many times I try bringing her back, it won't beat again.

Father
Jasper Kerkau

My father had a heart attack on a treadmill. He retired two weeks earlier. He lived to work. I lived a life of leisure waiting tables and drinking. I pulled up to the house I shared with friends and my sister was in my front yard crying. She didn't have to say anything. For a week we sat at the hospital, each in a different state of denial. *I felt his finger move that time.* I was too old to be waiting tables without a wife or a home of my own. My life was a failure. Deep shame. I would talk to his co-workers or relatives and see the look in their faces as I told them what I did—or rather, what I didn't do. Eventually it hit me. The shame and anguish of my life burst open as I realized that my father was already dead–he was a shell being kept alive by a machine. Shortly thereafter he was pronounced dead. My mother, sister, and I ate at a cafeteria and had an upbeat conversation and laughed. It wasn't funny but that is what people do sometimes in the face of tragedy—they laugh. Life wasn't funny for a long time after that. But, like anything, it eventually got better. I don't think about it now, his ashen face, his blue lips— the nothingness. Only periodically, when I work too much, does it come to my mind, I think about being sprawled out on the floor of a gym with strangers standing over me pumping my chest wildly, breathing in my mouth. Feeling the life slowly move out of my body. Sometimes the irony of life is perplexing.

Tempus fugit
Erich James Michaels

I imagined walking across the ocean floor
The immortal lobsters and jellyfish my friends
I said, "I wish I didn't have to breathe."
I thought of wasted time and dreams deferred
Of taking this split life and making it whole
I said, "I wish I didn't need to sleep."
I thought of money wasted, as hard to swallow
Of elevating myself above base needs
I said, "I wish I didn't need to eat."
I thought of myself as being set free
My life as a slave to the clock departed
She said, "Stop it! Why wish for death?"
Confused, I reflected on what I had said
Of what could be gained by being free of need
No need to breathe, sleep or eat
It was at that moment I realized
Just what I had really wished for

Surface Dweller
Laurie Wise

Prison of promises
Delusions for the damned
Lies and betrayal
Death comes in intervals
Layer upon layer
Until all that is left are
Living dead
Shuffling round my head
Knocking at the door
Needing more
Offering less
Say you will save me
Whispering I love you
Behind my back
Fingers crossed
Soul stealer
Contradictions collect
In cranial crevices
Where absurdity blurs
Redundant reality
Devil keeps me company
Tap tap tapping claws
On protruding spine
Reciting rhymes
Psalms of sacrifice
Fracturing fault lines
Interrupting time
Minutia mocks me
Days become weeks

Become months
Become hell on earth
Eroded
Dusted eyes
Search ashen skies
Stifling cries
Regurgitated hope
Assures every ending
Begets a new beginning
Rueful rebirth
I'm waiting
Gunpowder on my breath
Surface dwellers
Feign faith
While I die my last death

Can You Feel the Winter Coming?

Allie Nelson

Kneel for the Alfather, in standing stone,
bloody runes on the boulder and crawl in,
soak in mead and honey, tangle your hair,
it is golden in the dark cave, burn burn.
The firmament churns like Urd makes butter,
Frigga spins flax and cards heavenly wool,
I make rainbows out of Heimdall's breath,
but the Wild Hunt does not ride my Bifrost –
No, my path is for the dead, past Helheim,
in unions in darkest earthen cauldrons,
slick with the dew of Ymir's icy wastes,
I am alone in Ginnunungap, paltry salt.
I am Mordgud Blood Maiden, I am bell toll.
Watch me weave my arteries on my spine,
pay my ferrywoman price, tithe your Hel
I will offer you to Her, nothing more.
Nothing less than a table at Hela's dry
feet, the dust bread of dead, silence.
Down here it is cold but no one wants.
Down here it freezes, but we don't feel.
Can you see Her spread Her fingers aloft
in the vines of veins, veins of leaves,
ribs of trees, trees of the nine worlds?
Winter is coming, Odin does not own it.
Winter is coming, and Fenrir howls high.
The moon is eaten by wolves, the sun bleeds
gold then darkness in Hati's lupine womb,
plant seeds in beast's black after harvest.
Winter is here, Hela walks as ice maiden.

Autumn just a passing fancy, and Valraven
rots on a yew, corpse bloated and swinging,
in Dying He is more alive than the Living.
Know the secrets of Hela Half-Rotted, see
the pennants of flesh on her corpse breast,
smell the compost and dirt of Her skin, kiss
Her bone hand, and sleep until springtide.
Sleep, dream, die, it is all the same to me,
for I have dreamed and died and eaten ashes,
She was sweet to me, He was a thunder strike,
in autumn He and She make a secret only I know.
What is the secret of Bolverk and Loki's Pride?
It is sweet Balder on a shiply pyre adrift to
seidhr waters, golden Nanna enflamed, safety
is only found after Ragnarok, wouldn't you know?
Winter came for Balder come mistletoe's kiss.
And Odin rides the worlds for His son's ghost.
Sweet Frigga weeps tears of sapphire, then snow.
And Hela and Nanna talk long by the hearth-side.
Winter comes for us all, even the gods, even
Death will Die, and in Dying, Live Again,
Anew, Life Eternal may be found in snow.

Upon This Hill
Christine E. Ray

the pages of
the calendar
remain unchanged
old
outdated
too much effort
required
to remove it
from the wall
I no longer wear
a watch upon my
pale wrist
no need to measure
minutes
hours
by the passing
of a hand
before my face
hourglass sand
trickles grain by grain from
fractured glass bulb
onto the copper table
I write my name
upon the surface
a eulogy
time has gained
a boneless quality
become a black sea
I no longer swim in

a twilight land
where stunted sunflowers
dwarf versions
of their former selves
strain on anxious stalks
reach for stingy rays
of an indifferent sun
their petiolate leaves
grab hungrily
at my bare feet
calves
anchor me in place
I stand frozen
for an eternity
before I sink slowly
silently
into cool loam
my pockets
lined with pain
stuffed with
memory shards
fragments of dreams
the fragrance
of crushed rosemary
lemon balm
weigh me down
I am so tired
so very tired
it is so lovely here
I surrender
to the stillness
the peace
this moment offers

and I. . .
let go
my blood will
water these flowers
the calcium of my bones
will nourish this soil
tender new shoots
will wrap around the
trellis of my ribs
new life will
flourish here
butterflies
luna moths
adorn this burial mound

Two Seconds
Oldepunk

Above
looking down from
the edge of earth
there is a hole
in my chest
my essence is pouring out
nuances of memories and
the skeletons of dreams
no one seems to notice
there's a hole
in my chest
and you can see straight through me
put down in configuration
of paper mache´ and Indian dye
clutter surrounds the opening
I cannot seem to return
pieces to their origin
a grin, a sin, thought of a friend
who is falling through
the hole in my chest
entertaining landscape ebullient
tamp down edges
seal in bronze and copper
vast is all that comes to mind
2 seconds last eternity
I hear the thunder of Zeus
casting vengeance into the nether
dropped to my knees
I know not what to do

there is so much time
there is no time
the parade of echoes
rushing down my
stomach and thighs
merging with distance and gravity
i am forever, i am nothing
horses running wild in the visions
that hammer home a
stifling conclusion
a shocking bulletin
there is a
hole in my chest
I fall back, imploding through
the beginning
I recall womb-love
hearth and home
faces dear and
old stale fears
I am born again as I hear
my last words dropping from
the edge of the earth
"Help me, I think I've been shot"
I had died prior to having
the hole in my chest
It was a curious demise

I-float-until-I-am-hung / I-am-hanging-while-I-float

Aakriti Kuntal

You will often find me hanging loosely
Like structures of dust, under the mattress,
above the mattress, on the shelf, the window,
the bookrack, in the things I touch, in the things
I mirror

Mother said ' You should have died sooner '

I wonder if I should have plucked my naval
into a bleeding pool and draped the umbilical cord
around my paper
corset, a Sakura hangman's knot

I rinse my throat every morning as I enter the mirror
in my threaded bluish gown, my face cut and placed,
Like seismic continents sewn by beaded colors

I take the toothpaste and rub it onto my teeth, lest anyone
detect the stench from a failing me,
run my face under water,
a few hundred times, hoping my skin would grow ameba
feet
and hide inside the uterus of damp pipelines

Hoping then that all of me would follow
and I would be like a balloon gently massaging its belly
against lavender corns of air,
waistline glowing,

while a counter rested inside the crotch,
waiting to puncture all life

I watch the doctors arrive in their whitewashed suits and
surgical eyes, their occasional smiles disturbing
the atmosphere of possible murder,
The lights loom over my face as if to have a good hard
look,
as if to mock, once again

You will often find me hanging loosely
Like structures of dust, under the mattress,
above the mattress, on the shelf, the window,
the book rack, in the things I touched, in the things
that hold

i checked myself
Lois Linkens

i have checked myself and seen that i am nothing;
the bones of poets gone and done
lay beneath the hills.
i put on my boots and took my shovel,
for to disturb them
would be a lesser crime than to ignore.

i checked myself
and saw that i was nothing;
i looked for art
and saw it slither into bank accounts in dead of night,
while the dewy brows of poverty's poets
tremble in their plight.

i checked myself
and let myself stand up.
stand up, i said –
stand up, writers!
stand up for complexity, confusion and colour.
take your pennies and forget the pied pipers,
they have led naught but rats.

i saw the riches over realness,
splendour over solidarity…
i cried upon my pillow.
my people, my people!
when the muses so return, tell them why you wrote!

we not one of us free falls –

i checked myself...
something always had me.

Sudden Denouement Literary Collective

Kindra M. Austin
Michigan, USA
https://poemsandparagraphs.com/

Jimmi Campkin
Whitby, England
https://jimmicampkin.com/

Richard Crandall
Houston, Texas USA
https://superrobotparty.wordpress.com/

Sarah Doughty
Indianapolis, Indiana USA
https://thesarahdoughty.wordpress.com/ &
Instagram.com/thesarahdoughty

Matthew D. Eayre
Houston, Texas USA
https://unevenstreetstudios.com/ &
Instagram.com/matthew_d_eayre

Daffni Gingerich
Southeastern, Connecticut USA
https://daffniblog.wordpress.com/

Mitch Green
Alpharetta Georgia, USA
https://radpublishing.co &
Instagram.com/mitch_grn &
@radpresspublishing

Iulia Halatz
Bucharest, Romania
https://blogdecompanie.wordpress.com/

Mick Hugh
Asbury Park, NJ USA
https://micksneonfog.com/

Jasper Kerkau
Houston Texas
https://jasperkerkauwriting.com/

Ra'ahe Khayat
Mumbai, India
https://fallenalone.wordpress.com/

Aakriti Kuntal
Bengaluru, India
https://aakritikuntal.wordpress.com/ &
Instagram.com/blue_hemisphere/

Lois Linkens
England

David Lohrey
Tokyo, Japan
https://davlohrey.wordpress.com/

Samantha Lucero
USA
https://sixredseeds.wordpress.com/

Nicole Lyons
Canada

N. Ian McCarthy
USA
https://madbongomaze.wordpress.com/

Nathan McCool
USA
https://mistofmelancholia.wordpress.com/

Max Meunier
USA
https://maxmeunierpoetry.com/

Erich James Michaels
Fulton, New York USA
https://erichmichaels.wordpress.com

Allie Nelson
Washington, D.C. USA
https://dancewithtricksters.wordpress.com/

S. K. Nicholas
Bedfordshire, England
https://myredabyss.com/

Jonathan O'Farrell
Leicester, England
https://misterkaki.blog & https://misterkaki-writer.substack.com

Oldepunk
Arlingdingdondemdamdomton, Texas USA
https://ramjetpoetry.wordpress.com/

Georgia Park
Salem, MA
https://privatebadthoughts.com/

Christine E. Ray
Greater Philadelphia Area, Pennsylvania USA
https://braveandrecklessblog.com/

Henna Sjöblom
Finland
https://murdertrampbirthday.wordpress.com/

Marcia Weber
Dayton, OH USA
https://auroraphoenixdoc.wordpress.com

Laurie Wise
Pacific Northwest, USA
https://wisewoman2016.wordpress.com/

Made in the USA
Columbia, SC
25 June 2018